# The ASQ CQE Study Guide

Also available from ASQ Quality Press:

*The Certified Quality Engineer Handbook*, Third Edition
Connie M. Borror, editor

*The Certified Reliability Engineer Handbook*, Second Edition
Donald W. Benbow and Hugh W. Broome

*The Certified Quality Technician Handbook*, Second Edition
H. Fred Walker, Donald W. Benbow, and Ahmad K. Elshennawy

*The Certified Quality Inspector Handbook*, Second Edition
H. Fred Walker, Ahmad K. Elshennawy, Bhisham C. Gupta, and Mary McShane Vaughn

*Statistics for Six Sigma Black Belts*
Matthew Barsalou

*The Certified Six Sigma Black Belt Handbook*, Third Edition
T. M. Kubiak and Donald W. Benbow

*The Certified Six Sigma Master Black Belt Handbook*
T. M. Kubiak

*Practical Engineering, Process, and Reliability Statistics*
Mark Allen Durivage

*The Quality Toolbox*, Second Edition
Nancy R. Tague

*Root Cause Analysis: Simplified Tools and Techniques*, Second Edition
Bjørn Andersen and Tom Fagerhaug

*The Certified Manager of Quality/Organizational Excellence Handbook*, Fourth Edition
Russell T. Westcott, editor

*The ASQ Quality Improvement Pocket Guide: Basic History, Concepts, Tools, and Relationships*
Grace L. Duffy, editor

To request a complimentary catalog of ASQ Quality Press publications, call 800-248-1946, or visit our website at http://www.asq.org/quality-press.

# THE ASQ CQE STUDY GUIDE

*Connie M. Borror*
*Sarah E. Burke*

ASQ Quality Press
Milwaukee, Wisconsin

American Society for Quality, Quality Press, Milwaukee 53203
© 2016 by ASQ
All rights reserved. Published 2015
Printed in the United States of America
25 24 23 22 21 HP 12 11 10 9 8

**Library of Congress Cataloging-in-Publication Data**

Names: Borror, Connie M., author. | Burke, Sarah E. (Sarah Ellen), 1989–
    author. | American Society for Quality.
Title: The ASQ CQE study guide / Connie M. Borror and Sarah E. Burke.
Description: Milwaukee, Wisconsin : ASQ Quality Press, 2015. | Includes index.
Identifiers: LCCN 2015039810 | ISBN 9780873899192 (soft cover ring bound :
    alk. paper)
Subjects:  LCSH: Quality control—Examinations—Study guides.
Classification: LCC TS156 .B658 2015 | DDC 658.4/013—dc23
LC record available at http://lccn.loc.gov/2015039810

ISBN: 978-0-87389-919-2

# Table of Contents

# Introduction

This book is primarily meant to aid those taking the ASQ Certified Quality Engineer (CQE) exam and is best used in conjunction with *The Certified Quality Engineer Handbook* (ASQ Quality Press). Section 1 provides 380 practice questions organized by the seven parts of the 2015 Body of Knowledge (BoK). Section 2 gives the reader 205 additional practice questions from each of the seven parts, in a randomized order.

For every question in both sections, detailed solutions are provided that explain why each answer is the correct one and also which section of the BoK the question corresponds to so that any further study needed can be focused on specific sections.

A secondary audience is those taking exams for ASQ certifications whose BoKs' have some crossover with the CQE. Namely, the Certified Six Sigma Black Belt (CSSBB), Certified Six Sigma Green Belt (CSSGB), Certified Reliability Engineer (CRE), and Certified Quality Inspector (CQI). Using this guide in studying for any of these exams would be extremely useful, particularly for the statistics portions of the BoKs.

Unlike other resources on the market, all these questions and solutions were developed specifically to address the 2015 CQE Body of Knowledge and help those studying for it, including taking into account the proper depth of knowledge and required levels of cognition. None of this material has appeared in any previous resource or been shoehorned into fitting under the BoK's topics.

As a reminder, practice/sample test questions such as those in this study guide can not be taken into ASQ certification exam rooms. The exams are open book, though, so it is highly recommended that you do take *The Certified Quality Engineer Handbook* in with you to look up or verify any answers as you work the exam questions.

We welcome your feedback and suggestions for improvement. Please contact us at authors@asq.org and we will do our best to clarify any questions you may have and incorporate any suggestions for improvement into future printings or editions of this study guide.

Connie M. Borror
Sarah E. Burke

# Section 1
## Sample Questions by BoK

Section 1 is divided into seven parts, one for each section in the Certified Quality Engineer Body of Knowledge. In each part, there is a set of questions followed by detailed solutions.

# Part I
## Management and Leadership

(30 questions)

## QUESTIONS

1. A system improvement program based on the philosophy that one or more factors prevents a system from reaching a more desirable state is:

   a. Lean Six Sigma.

   b. Six Sigma.

   c. lean.

   d. theory of constraints.

2. Which of the following is *not* part of the original Juran trilogy for quality?

   a. Quality audit

   b. Quality control

   c. Quality planning

   d. Quality improvement

3. According to the Juran trilogy, quality improvement is:

   a. monitoring techniques to correct sporadic problems.

   b. an annual quality program to institutionalize managerial control and review.

   c. a method that drives out fear so that everyone may work effectively.

   d. a breakthrough sequence to solve chronic problems.

4. Which of the following is one of Deming's 14 points?

   a. Eliminate work standards that prescribe numerical quotas.

   b. Institute barriers that stand between the hourly worker and his right to pride of workmanship.

    c. 85% of quality problems are due to the system.

    d. 15% of quality problems are due to management.

5. Quality defined as "fitness for use" is attributed to:

    a. Deming

    b. Crosby

    c. Feigenbaum

    d. Juran

6. SWOT is the acronym for:

    a. strengths, weaknesses, outcomes, and threats.

    b. strengths, weaknesses, opportunities, and threats.

    c. suppliers, workers, opportunities, and tables.

    d. strengths, weaknesses, opportunities, and tables.

7. Which of the following would be considered an effectiveness test for strategic planning?

    a. Have modern methods of training on the job been instituted?

    b. Have only those people who have experience in a particular job position been hired?

    c. Are the goals and objectives aligned throughout the organization?

    d. None of the above

8. In strategic planning, SMART represents:

    a. strengths, machines, applications, realistic, and time-based.

    b. strengths, measurable, achievable, realistic, and threats.

    c. specific, measurable, achievable, realistic, and time-based.

    d. specific, measurable, applications, reliability, and time-based.

9. Critical path method (CPM) is:

    a. a project management technique.

    b. part of the Kano quality model.

    c. one of Deming's 14 points.

    d. Juran's model for quality improvement.

10. Action plans as part of the goals and objectives of a deployment technique are:

    a. to continually build and retain a loyal customer base.

    b. to deliver all products to all customers 100% on time.

    c. detailed plans stating how, when, and by whom the objective will be achieved.

    d. None of the above

11. The process organizations use to evaluate their performance against their competition or best practices found internally is referred to as:

    a. benchmarking.

    b. CPM.

    c. deployment.

    d. stakeholder analysis.

12. Benchmarking projects will include the following steps:

    a. Planning, detection, analysis, and implementation.

    b. Planning, data collection, analysis, and implementation.

    c. Promotion, detection, analysis, and implementation.

    d. Promotion, data collection, analysis, and planning.

13. The owners of a company are the:

    a. stockholders.

    b. executive group.

    c. suppliers.

    d. customers.

14. Performance measures:

    a. should be achievable.

    b. do not need to be measurable.

    c. do not need to be linked to strategic objectives.

    d. should focus on as many measures as possible.

15. The four perspectives of a "balanced scorecard" proposed by Kaplan and Norton do not include:

    a.  business processes.

    b.  customers.

    c.  stockholders.

    d.  financial fundamentals.

16. Which of the following tools can be used for justifying and prioritizing projects?

    a.  Net present value

    b.  Payback period

    c.  Internal rate of return

    d.  All of the above

17. Suppose we estimate the net present value (NPV) for a particular project. When we want to determine how the NPV will change if the interest rate decreases or increases, for example, by 5%, we are doing a type of:

    a.  decision tree analysis.

    b.  internal rate of return analysis.

    c.  payback period analysis.

    d.  sensitivity analysis.

18. A Gantt chart is a useful:

    a.  financial tool.

    b.  planning tool.

    c.  statistical analysis tool.

    d.  None of the above

19. What method allows for the analysis of normal time to complete a task and analysis of the longest timeline to complete a project?

    a.  Critical path method

    b.  Program evaluation and review technique

    c.  A Gantt chart

    d.  None of the above

20. Which of the following is a use of a quality information system?

    a. Control a process

    b. Monitor a process

    c. Record critical data

    d. a and b only

    e. a, b, and c

21. Which of the following is not one of the sections of the ASQ Code of Ethics?

    a. Fundamental Principles

    b. Relations with the Public

    c. Quality Information Systems

    d. Relations with Peers

22. Common development stages teams often progress through are known as *forming, storming, norming,* and *performing.* In the "storming" stage:

    a. individuals begin to shift from personal concerns to the needs of the team.

    b. the team's mission is clarified and specific roles are identified.

    c. team members still think and act as individuals instead of impacting as a team.

    d. the team has matured and is working in the best interest of the team and team goals.

23. Keeping the team on task is the main function of the:

    a. team leader.

    b. facilitator.

    c. team note taker.

    d. None of the above

24. Part of the team facilitator's mission is to:

    a. discuss content issues with the team.

    b. discuss process issues with the team.

    c. suggest technical solutions to the team.

    d. None of the above

25. A useful brainstorming tool for reducing a large list of items to a smaller, manageable one is:

    a. quality function deployment.

    b. fault tree analysis.

    c. nominal group technique.

    d. operating characteristic curve.

26. In the communication process, there are five methods of feedback: evaluation, interpretation, support, probing, and understanding. Of these methods, the one that most often creates defensiveness and can quickly break the communication process is:

    a. evaluation.

    b. support.

    c. probing.

    d. understanding.

27. A planning technique that translates customer requirements into technical requirements is:

    a. benchmarking.

    b. SWOT.

    c. customer satisfaction surveys.

    d. quality function deployment.

28. "House of quality" is a key diagram in:

    a. quality function deployment.

    b. flowcharts.

    c. PERT.

    d. CPM.

29. The purpose of surveying a supplier is to determine if the supplier has:

    a. adequate financial resources.

    b. adequate manufacturing capabilities.

    c. adequate quality systems.

   d.  All of the above

   e.  None of the above

30. Implementing quality improvement in an organization can be a failure for a number of reasons. Which of the following is one obstacle to implementing quality?

   a.  Lack of real employee empowerment

   b.  Lack of a formal strategic plan for change

   c.  Lack of strong motivation

   d.  All of the above are obstacles.

   e.  None of the above are obstacles.

## SOLUTIONS

1.  d; Theory of constraints focuses on the system processes that keep the entire system from working at an improved state. Lean focuses on eliminating waste, while Six Sigma emphasizes minimizing variability. [I.A.2]

2.  a; Juran understood that improving quality required different approaches and effort than simply maintaining quality. The Juran trilogy focused on three philosophies: quality planning, quality control, and quality improvement. Although auditing is one tool emphasized, it is not considered an overarching philosophy. [I.A.1]

3.  d; In his 1964 text, *Managerial Breakthrough*, Juran defined quality improvement as a breakthrough sequence to solve chronic problems that is analogous to "common causes." [I.A.1]

4.  a; Deming argued that work standards that include numerical quotas do nothing to motivate the common worker and should be eliminated. [I.A.1]

5.  d; Juran. [I.A.2]

6.  b; SWOT analysis (strengths, weaknesses, opportunities, and threats) is conducted to assess strengths and weaknesses of an organization, to predict opportunities, and to identify threats from competitors. [I.B.1]

7.  c; a and b are two of Deming's 14 points; goals and objectives aligned throughout the organization are necessary to carry out the strategies to be put in place. [I.B.1]

8.  c; Goals and objectives should be "specific, measurable, achievable, realistic, and time-based" to be effective throughout the enterprise. [I.B.1]

9. a; CPM is a project management technique used for resource planning. [I.B.2.d]

10. c; Action plans often resemble mini project plans, or more-complex project planning documents may be in order. [I.B.2]

11. a; Benchmarking is the process by which companies compare their processes against best practices found either internally or externally. [I.B.2.a]

12. b; Typically, benchmarking projects must have a plan, data must be collected for analysis, and finally, implementation of results of the analysis. [I.B.2.a]

13. a; The stockholders of a company are considered the owners of the company. Their role is of a financial nature, but generally passive. [I.B.2.b]

14. a; All performance measures should be achievable and aligned with strategic goals. In addition, the focus should be on the "vital few." One should avoid using too many measures or metrics. [I.B.2.c]

15. c; Stockholders are not a direct perspective of a balanced scorecard and its uses. [I.B.2.b]

16. d; All three methods are sometimes used for justifying and prioritizing projects. [I.B.2.d]

17. d; When metrics are examined by varying the inputs (such as percentage, rate, and so on) in NPV, we are conducting a sensitivity analysis. [I.B.2.d]

18. b; A Gantt chart is also a milestone chart—a planning tool. [I.B.2.d]

19. a; Critical path method (CPM) chart. [I.B.2.d]

20. e; a, b, and c are all uses of a quality information system. [I.B.3]

21. c; The other three answers are each on of the three sections of the ASQ Code of Ethics. [I.C]

22. c; In the storming phase, teams become familiar with one another, have worked on missions and strategies, but often are still working in the individuals' best interests and not necessarily the team's as a whole. [I.D]

23. b; The facilitator's role is to provide support for the team, and the main task for that individual is to keep the team on task. [I.E.1]

24. b; The facilitator's role should be marginal and grow less important as the team matures. Overall, the facilitator is responsible for process issues—meeting agendas, communication among teams, and keeping the team on task. [I.E.1]

25. c; The nominal group technique allows for brainstorming a large number of ideas/suggestions while providing everyone an equal voice in the process. [I.E.2]

26. a; All feedback methods can lead to a breakdown in the communication process. However, evaluation, which involves a judgment being made about the importance, worth, or appropriateness of the statement, is the one that will lead to a breakdown much more quickly. It will also take a great deal of effort to recover from such feedback. [I.F]

27. d; QFD is a powerful tool for incorporating the voice of the customer and identifying the necessary technical requirements that will be necessary to satisfy customer requirements. [I.G]

28. a; The house of quality is a diagram that incorporates the key relationships in the process. [I.G]

29. d; Surveying and auditing the supplier are not the same activity. The purpose of the survey of a supplier or potential supplier is to make sure their financial resources as well as their manufacturing capabilities and quality systems are acceptable. These three arenas are surveyed by appropriate groups involved with each particular activity (manufacturing capability surveyed by manufacturing engineer, for example). [I.H]

30. d; The *CQE Handbook* (3rd edition) provides an overview of 12 common barriers or obstacles to a successful implementation of quality improvement in an organization: lack of time to devote to quality initiatives, poor intraorganizational communication, lack of real employee empowerment, lack of employee trust in senior management, politics and turf issues, lack of a formalized strategic plan for change, lack of strong motivation, view of quality as a quick fix, drive for short-term financial results, lack of leadership, lack of customer focus, lack of a company-wide definition of quality. [I.I]

# Part II
## The Quality System

(31 questions)

## QUESTIONS

1. For any quality system, all quality-related activities begin with:

    a. sales and distribution.

    b. process planning.

    c. customer needs.

    d. product design.

2. A quality manual generally consists of four *tiers* or *layers* that include:

    a. policies, procedures, instructions, and records.

    b. policies, documentation, instructions, and records.

    c. documentation, implementation, compliance, and accuracy.

    d. compliance, accuracy, clarity, and records.

3. The critical characteristics of any documentation of a quality system are:

    a. compliance, implementation, and clarity.

    b. compliance, clarity, and procedures.

    c. procedures, accuracy, and clarity.

    d. compliance, accuracy, and clarity.

4. One major component of a quality system is:

    a. supplier management.

    b. implementation of a documented quality system.

    c. contractor assessment.

    d. auditing of suppliers.

Part II
Questions

5. Once a quality manual is complete, a final review is in order. The reviewed copy should be endorsed and authorized for release by:

   a. suppliers.

   b. customers.

   c. top management.

   d. the chief quality officer.

6. Which of the following is not a requirement for maintaining document control?

   a. A process is in place for distribution of revisions and removal of obsolete documents.

   b. A process is in place for making the documents readily available to the general public.

   c. A process ensures that documents are located so they are readily available where needed.

   d. A process is in place for the generation, approval, and distribution of documents.

7. ISO 9001:2015 is:

   a. a national standard.

   b. an international standard.

   c. an industry-specific standard.

   d. None of the above

8. Which of the following is *not* one of the standards in the ISO 9000 Quality Management Systems family?

   a. *Fundamentals and Vocabulary*

   b. *Continual Improvement*

   c. *Requirements*

   d. *Guidelines for Performance*

9. The ISO 9000 series of standards emphasizes eight quality management principles. Which of the following would be categorized as one of those principles?

   a. Understanding customer needs

   b. Use of technical language in all technical descriptions

    c. Use of different terms and vocabulary

    d. None of the above

10. Which of the following ISO standards are *not* requirements, but guidelines only?

    a. ISO 9000

    b. ISO 9001

    c. ISO 9004

    d. All of the above are requirements.

11. The Malcolm Baldrige National Quality Award consists of how many key criteria for performance excellence?

    a. 14

    b. 8

    c. 7

    d. 4

12. A quality audit is to be conducted within a particular company. An employee of this company will be conducting the audit. This is an example of:

    a. an internal quality audit.

    b. an external quality audit.

    c. a third-party quality audit.

    d. None of the above

13. The most comprehensive type of audit is the:

    a. quality system audit.

    b. product quality audit.

    c. process quality audit.

    d. service quality audit.

14. Which of the following would be a purpose for a quality audit?

    a. To meet requirements for certification to a management standard

    b. Verification of conformance with contractual requirements

    c. To contribute to the improvement of the management system

    d. All of the above are reasons for a quality audit.

15. A quality audit has been conducted and some corrective measures are recommended. The party responsible for planning and implementing these measures is:

    a.  the auditee.

    b.  the lead auditor.

    c.  management where the corrective measures are needed.

    d.  line workers where the corrective measures are needed.

16. Corrective action and verification that nonconformities have been addressed is:

    a.  always carried out.

    b.  often poorly completed.

    c.  unnecessary and causes more stress than it is worth.

    d.  None of the above

17. The lead auditor must explain to the auditee the objectives of the audit as well as the methods that will be used. This is usually done during:

    a.  the opening meeting (or pre-examination).

    b.  the closing meeting.

    c.  the audit itself.

    d.  It is not necessary for the auditor to explain this information to the auditee.

18. Who is responsible for the accuracy of the final audit report?

    a.  Auditee

    b.  Client

    c.  Lead auditor

    d.  None of the above

19. The auditee will begin improvement efforts to address any problems or corrections identified by the audit. A follow-up audit to verify results of this improvement effort:

    a.  should be agreed on by all parties: client, auditor, auditee.

    b.  is not necessary or recommended.

    c.  is conducted by someone in the company when there is time.

    d.  None of the above

20. A company increased prevention costs by making changes to its quality control area, and then nonconformities decreased. As a result, there was a reduction in:

    a. operating costs.

    b. appraisal costs.

    c. failure costs.

    d. quality costs.

21. Correction of data entry errors, specimen processing, and cost of reeducating staff in a laboratory before delivery of the results to the customer are examples of:

    a. prevention costs.

    b. appraisal costs.

    c. internal failure costs.

    d. external failure costs.

22. In one year, the cost of proficiency testing for quality assurance by an external certified agency for all employees was $10,000. This cost would be categorized as:

    a. prevention cost.

    b. appraisal cost.

    c. internal failure cost.

    d. external failure cost.

23. Money spent on review of suppliers is:

    a. prevention cost.

    b. appraisal cost.

    c. external failure cost.

    d. internal failure cost.

24. As failure costs decrease, what typically happens to appraisal activities?

    a. Appraisal activities increase.

    b. Appraisal activities decrease.

    c. There is no relationship between the two.

    d. Appraisal activities will remain the same.

25. Test equipment depreciation is an example of:

    a.  prevention cost.

    b.  appraisal cost.

    c.  external failure cost.

    d.  internal failure cost.

26. Last month, a local company reported the following quality costs.

| Training | $40,000 |
|---|---|
| Material inspection | $12,000 |
| Test equipment | $65,000 |
| In-plant scrap and rework | $15,000 |

What is the total appraisal cost for last month?

    a.  $12,000

    b.  $92,000

    c.  $77,000

    d.  $65,000

27. Last month, a local company reported the following quality costs.

| Training | $40,000 |
|---|---|
| Material inspection | $12,000 |
| Test equipment | $65,000 |
| In-plant scrap and rework | $15,000 |

What is the external failure cost for last month?

    a.  $12,000

    b.  $92,000

    c.  $77,000

    d.  No external failure cost was reported.

28. A quality system audit is to be conducted. This is an example of a(n):

   a. prevention cost.

   b. appraisal cost.

   c. external failure cost.

   d. internal failure cost.

29. The first step in developing a training program is:

   a. design and development of the curriculum, or training plan.

   b. developing the lesson plan.

   c. conducting a pretest for the participants.

   d. assessing the need for the training.

30. Which of the following is *not* a reason for failure of a training program?

   a. Inadequacy of the leader/trainer.

   b. Different knowledge levels of the participants.

   c. Training is problem oriented rather than technique oriented.

   d. Overly complex language.

31. Pretests and posttests are useful tools in a training program for:

   a. assessing learning and retention.

   b. assessing the learner's reaction to training.

   c. identifying the weakest employees.

   d. None of the above

## SOLUTIONS

1. c; Throughout the product life cycle, understanding and identifying customer needs is the first and most important step in any quality-related activity. [II.A.1]

2. a; The four tiers are *policies*, *procedures*, *instructions*, and *records*. The first or top tier represents policies. The second tier represents procedures. The third tier represents work instructions. The fourth tier represents a record of results of implementing a quality system. [II.B.1]

3. d; Compliance, accuracy, and clarity; without these components, users will lose confidence in the documentation. [II.B.1]

4. b; Effective implementation of a quality system that has been reviewed and approved for release is one of the two major components of a quality program. The other component is documentation of procedures and instructions of the quality system. [II.A.1]

5. c; Top management is responsible for endorsing the content of the final document as well as authorizing its release for use. [II.B.2]

6. b; Documents do not have to be made readily available to the general public. [II.B.2]

7. b; ISO 9001:2015 is an international standard. [II.C]

8. b; Continual improvement is not one of the standards, but one of the eight quality management principles emphasized in the standard. [II.C]

9. a; Customer focus is a key quality management principle emphasized in the ISO 9000 family. Choices b and c refer to criteria for all ISO 9000 terms and definitions—and are illustrations of what not to do. In writing terms and definitions, technical definitions should be avoided, and coherent vocabulary agreed on and understood by all users (current and potential). [II.C]

10. c; ISO 9004 consists of suggestions only, guidelines but not requirements for certification. [II.C]

11. c; There are seven criteria: Leadership; Strategic Planning; Customer and Market Focus; Measurement, Analysis, and Knowledge Management; Human Resource Focus; Process Management; and Business/Organizational Performance Results. [II.C]

12. a; If the auditor is an employee of the company to be audited, then we refer to this as an *internal* audit. It is necessary that the person who will conduct this audit is not related to or involved in the activity that is being audited. [II.D.1]

13. a; A quality system audit is an audit of the entire system. The other three are more specific and smaller in scope. [II.D.1]

14. d; All of the choices are purposes for quality audits. A fourth purpose is to obtain and maintain confidence in the capability of a supplier. [II.D.1]

15. a; The organization or company being audited (auditee) is responsible for making sure the corrective measures identified are addressed. [II.D.2]

16. b; Actually taking corrective action when nonconformities have been identified is the one step in the process that is most often poorly executed. [II.D.3]

17. a; Generally, an audit is carried out in three steps: (1) pre-examination—the auditor explains the objectives of the audit, introduces team members to senior

management, and so on; (2) a "suitability" audit is conducted—comparison of documented procedures to the reference standard selected; and (3) implementation of the quality system is examined in depth, which may involve recommending corrective measures. [II.D.3].

18. c; The lead auditor is responsible for the accuracy as well as the validity of the final report. [II.D.2]

19. a; A follow-up audit is necessary to determine whether the problems and recommended corrections have been addressed. All three parties should arrange and agree on a follow-up audit. [II.D.4]

20. c; An increase in prevention costs, resulting in a decrease in defects, nonconformities, and so on, will result in a decrease in failure costs due to the reduction of defects and nonconformities. [II.E]

21. c; Since the data error correction, reprocessing, and reeducation occur before delivery of the product or service, the cost incurred would be an *internal* failure cost. [II.E]

22. b; Costs associated with activities performed to uncover or identify deficiencies (such as in personnel proficiency) are considered *appraisal* costs. [II.E]

23. a; Costs associated with activities related to supplier reviews are known as *prevention* costs. [II.E]

24. b; As failures are uncovered and corrected, appraisal activities will generally decrease, although appraisal activities will not and should not be completely eliminated. The type of appraisal activity can change. [II.E]

25. b; [II.E]

26. c; The items that would be considered for appraisal costs include test equipment and material inspection, so cost would be $12,000 + $65,000 = $77,000. [II.E]

27. d; None of the costs listed are external failure costs. In-plant scrap and rework is an internal failure cost. [II.E]

28. a; Quality system audits fall under prevention costs. [II.E]

29. d; Before developing and implementing any training program, a needs analysis should be conducted to determine whether the training is actually needed and, if so, what it should consist of. [II.F]

30. c; Frank Gryna noted that it was best if the participants could apply the training during the course to a problem of interest (be problem oriented). [II.F]

31. a; Pretests and posttests can be very useful for determining participant learning and retention of material. [II.F]

# Part III
## Product, Process, and Service Design

### (47 questions)

## QUESTIONS

1. Which of the following quality characteristics is an *attribute*?

    a. Body temperature

    b. Number of defects

    c. Length of a bolt

    d. Width of a board

2. A part will be inspected using a limit gage. An acceptable part is one that:

    a. mates with both ends of the limit gage (both "go" and "no-go").

    b. mates only with the "no-go" end of the gage.

    c. mates with neither end of the limit gage.

    d. mates with only the "go" end of the limit gage.

3. A system has two components in parallel, each with a reliability of 0.95. The system reliability is approximately:

    a. 0.9999.

    b. 0.9500.

    c. 0.9975.

    d. 0.0975.

4. Consider the product/process development life cycle. The phase in which the product or process is released to the customer for use is referred to as the:

    a. prototype phase.

    b. production phase.

    c. distribution phase.

    d. normal use phase.

5. Consider the product/process development life cycle. The phase in which all possible solutions are explored is referred to as the:

   a. specification phase.

   b. prototype phase.

   c. concept phase.

   d. distribution phase.

6. A tool that is useful for converting customer needs into design concepts is:

   a. process validation.

   b. quality function deployment.

   c. statistical process control.

   d. acceptance sampling.

7. Design reviews should be conducted by:

   a. top management only.

   b. a quality engineer.

   c. a cross-functional team including quality, manufacturing, and suppliers, and so on.

   d. customers only.

8. For each design review conducted, there are many different points of view from which the design should be considered. One of these viewpoints is from a reliability standpoint. Which of the following would be a question from a reliability viewpoint?

   a. Can the design be sufficiently tested?

   b. Is the failure rate acceptably low?

   c. Can the product be shipped without damage?

   d. Can the parts needed for the design be obtained at an acceptable cost?

9. A specification is given as $8^{+0.05/-0.05}$. The limits for this specification are:

   a. 8.00 and 8.05

   b. 7.95 and 8.00

   c. 7.95 and 8.05

   d. 8.05

10. Consider the following control frame.

| ⟋⟋ | Ⓛ | 0.01 | A | B | C |
|---|---|---|---|---|---|

0.01 represents the:

a. primary datum.

b. geometric feature or characteristic.

c. geometric tolerance.

d. modifier.

11. Consider the following control frame.

| ⟋⟋ | Ⓛ | 0.01 | A | B | C |
|---|---|---|---|---|---|

"A" represents the:

a. primary datum.

b. secondary datum.

c. tertiary datum.

d. modifier.

12. Which of the following involves demonstrating that all equipment being used in a process has been installed properly (as per manufacturer's specifications)?

a. Installation qualification

b. Operational qualification

c. Performance qualification

d. Software qualification

13. For a process, confirming that *specified* requirements have been fulfilled is known as:

a. validation.

b. verification.

c. qualification.

d. performance.

Part III
Questions

14. Validation of a product, process, or service is normally carried out:

   a.  during production or development.

   b.  when customer requirements are determined.

   c.  after completion of the product, process, or service.

   d.  None of the above

15. The *design for X* concept that focuses on eliminating problems before they occur is known as:

   a.  Design for reliability.

   b.  Design for cost.

   c.  Design for manufacturability.

   d.  Design for Six Sigma.

16. True/False. The reliability of a product can be measured at its release time.

   a.  True

   b.  False

17. The cumulative distribution function of failure at time $t$ for a type of air conditioner is defined as $F(t) = 4/5000$. Which of the following statements is (are) true?

   a.  The probability that a randomly selected air conditioner fails by time $t$ is 4/5000.

   b.  The probability that a randomly selected air conditioner will instantly fail is 4/5000.

   c.  The fraction of all units in the lot of air conditioners that fail by time $t$ is 4/5000.

   d.  a and c only.

   e.  All of the above

18. The cumulative distribution function of failure at time $t$ for a computer model is 0.992. What fraction of this computer model fails by time $t$?

   a.  0.992

   b.  0.008

c.  1

d.  None of the above

19. Which of the following probability distributions is the only one to have a constant failure rate?

   a.  Uniform

   b.  Normal

   c.  Exponential

   d.  Weibull

Use the following information for questions 20–22.

450 electrical components for a machine were subjected to a reliability test. The observed failures during 100-hour intervals are shown in the following table.

| Upper bound (hours) | Number of failures, $x$ |
|---|---|
| 0 | 0 |
| 100 | 7 |
| 200 | 16 |
| 300 | 19 |
| 400 | 27 |

20. What is the estimated reliability at time $t = 200$?

   a.  0.0156

   b.  0.9489

   c.  0.0511

   d.  0.0004

21. What is the estimated failure density for time $300 < t < 400$?

   a.  0.0006

   b.  0.9067

   c.  0.0933

   d.  0.8467

22. What is the instantaneous rate of failure for time $300 < t < 400$?

    a. 0.90667

    b. 0.09333

    c. 0.15333

    d. 0.00066

23. A series system is composed of five subsystems, each with reliability 0.995. What is the reliability of the system?

    a. 0.9950

    b. 0.9999

    c. 0.9752

    d. None of the above

24. A parallel system is composed of five subsystems, each with reliability 0.995. The reliability of this system is closest to which of the following values?

    a. 0.9950

    b. 1.0000

    c. 0.9752

    d. None of the above

25. True/False. In a parallel system, if one subsystem fails, the entire system will fail.

    a. True

    b. False

26. True/False. The reliability of a series system is lower than its weakest subsystem.

    a. True

    b. False

27. A machine has six subsystems and will fail when four or more of these subsystems fail. Each subsystem has a reliability of 0.88. What is the reliability of the machine?

    a. 0.5997

    b. 0.4644

    c. 0.9998

    d. 0.9975

28. A machine has a standby system design with four identical components in standby mode. Each component has a constant rate of failure $\lambda = 0.08$. What is the reliability of the machine at 100 hours of continuous operation?

   a.  0.9999

   b.  0.0001

   c.  0.0424

   d.  0.7164

29. 750 machines were tested for five hours. 28 failures occurred. What is the failure rate for these machines?

   a.  133

   b.  0.037

   c.  27

   d.  0.0075

30. The reliability of a component at $t = 400$ hours is 0.645. Assuming that the reliability of this component is exponential, which of the following is closest to the mean time to failure (MTTF)?

   a.  0.0011

   b.  910

   c.  0.355

   d.  3

31. The MTTF for a model of dishwasher is 115 months. What is the reliability that a randomly selected dishwasher of this model type survives past 115 months? Assume that the reliability function is an exponential distribution.

   a.  0.368

   b.  2.718

   c.  0.009

   d.  0.632

32. The MTTF for a machine is 525 hours. What fraction of machines survives past 1000 hours? Assume that the reliability of the machine has an exponential distribution.

   a.  85.12%

b.  14.88%

c.  0.19%

d.  99.81%

33. What is the probability a randomly selected rechargeable battery fails by six hours if the mean time between failures (MTBF) is five hours? Assume that the reliability of the component is exponentially distributed.

  a.  0.3012

  b.  0.1667

  c.  0.8333

  d.  0.6988

34. If the MTBF of a component is 900 hours, what is the reliability of this component at 500 hours? Assume that the reliability of the component is exponentially distributed.

  a.  0.1653

  b.  0.8347

  c.  0.4262

  d.  0.5738

35. The failure rate of a machine is 0.0008. Assuming the life distribution of this type of machine is exponential, what fraction of machines in the population survives longer than the MTTF?

  a.  36.79%

  b.  63.21%

  c.  1250

  d.  99.92%

36. The failure rate of a machine is 0.0008. Assuming the life distribution of this type of machine is exponential and the MTTF is five hours, what is the steady-state availability of this machine?

  a.  0.004

  b.  1250

  c.  0.996

  d.  1255

37. In a test of a repairable component of a machine, 600 components were tested for 25 hours and 515 components failed. If the mean time to repair (MTTR) these components is eight hours, what is the steady-state availability of this component?

    a. 29.13

    b. 0.2155

    c. 0.7845

    d. 0.0343

38. Which type of maintenance policy allows for the maximum run time between repairs?

    a. Preventive maintenance policy

    b. Corrective maintenance policy

    c. Predictive maintenance policy

    d. None of the above

39. A preventive maintenance policy is recommended if:

    a. the cost to repair the system after its failure is less than the cost of maintaining the system before its failure.

    b. the failure rate of the function of the system is monotonically increasing.

    c. the cost to repair the system after its failure is greater than the cost of maintaining the system before its failure.

    d. both b and c.

    e. None of the above

40. In the second region identified in the general failure rate model (the bathtub curve), what is the most common cause for failures?

    a. The manufacturing process

    b. Fatigue

    c. Random failures

    d. All of the above

41. Which of the following probability distributions is often used to model the second region of the bathtub curve?

    a. Uniform

b.  Weibull

c.  Exponential

d.  Normal

42. Which of the following probability distributions is often used to model the third region of the bathtub curve?

a.  Uniform

b.  Weibull

c.  Exponential

d.  Normal

43. What is the main goal of FMEA?

a.  To help reduce the negative effects of potential failures before they occur

b.  To organize the workplace environment

c.  To communicate hierarchical relationships between events

d.  To reduce the number of defects produced in a process

44. A hospital is preparing to do an FMEA for a surgical procedure. Which of the following groups of employees should make up the FMEA team members?

a.  One doctor that performs this surgical procedure

b.  A nurse and doctor

c.  A doctor, nurse, technician, engineer, business office employee, and manager

d.  None of the above

45. Which of the following are components of an FMEA?

a.  Potential failure modes

b.  The risk associated with potential failures

c.  Corrective action plans

d.  All of the above

46. An FMEA team has identified a potential failure and assessed the following score for severity, occurrence, and detection for this failure mode: 8, 2, 6. What is the RPN for this failure mode?

a.  16

b.  8

c.  96

d.  None of the above

47. What is the main goal of an FMECA?

a.  To reduce the number of defects produced in a process.

b.  To develop a prioritization scheme for corrective action plans.

c.  To organize the workplace environment.

d.  To communicate hierarchical relationships between events.

## SOLUTIONS

1.  b; A *defect* is an attribute. Either the defect is present or it is not. A defect has no real measurement on a continuous scale. [III.A]

2.  d; An acceptable part should only fit within the "go" end of the limit gage. If it passes on both ends, it is an unacceptable part. [III.A]

3.  c; For components in parallel, each with reliability of $p$, the system reliability is given by $R_s(t) = 1 - (1 - p)^2 = 1 - (1 - 0.95)^2 = 0.9975$. [III.E.2]

4.  d; The *normal use phase* of the development life cycle includes release of the product/process to the customer for its intended use or function. Normal wear and maintenance occur in this phase as well. [III.B.1]

5.  c; In the concept phase, all possible solutions are explored. Nonfeasible solutions are eliminated. [III.B.1]

6.  b; QFD, which uses the "house of quality," is helpful in turning customer needs into product characteristics or design concepts. [III.B.1]

7.  c; Because of the complexity of design reviews, a cross-functional team consisting of many different personnel should conduct the review. The team should include, but not be limited to, quality personnel, manufacturing, suppliers, customers, and so on. [III.B.1]

8.  b; Reliability includes metrics such as failure rates for the design under consideration. [III.B.1]

9.  c; This is a bilateral tolerance with allowable variation in both directions. [III.C]

10. c; 0.01 represents the geometric tolerance for the feature on the part. [III.C]

11. a; "A" represents the primary datum. [III.C]

12. a; Installation qualification. The goal is to make sure the equipment involved is installed properly. [III.D]

13. b; Verification deals with determining whether the product or process satisfies specified requirements, that is, it meets all specifications or requirements. But this does not guarantee that the product or process specifications meet or exceed predetermined requirements (that is, it may not work like it is supposed to). [III.D]

14. c; Validation takes place after the product, process, or service is finished or completed. Validation is used to determine whether predetermined requirements are being met (product/process/service is working as intended). [III.D]

15. d; Design for Six Sigma is an approach used to eliminate problems before they occur. [III.B.2]

16. b; Reliability can not be measured at the release time of the product; it can only be predicted. This is because the reliability of a product is dependent on many factors, including the system design, the reliability of its components, the operating environment, environmental factors, and manufacturing defects. [III.E.1]

17. d; The cumulative distribution function (cdf) of failure $F(t)$ has two interpretations: (1) the probability that a randomly selected unit from the population will fail by time $t$, or (2) the fraction of all units in the population that fail by time $t$. The hazard rate function $h(t)$ defines the instantaneous failure rate at time $t$. [III.E.1]

18. a; The cumulative distribution function (cdf) of failure can be interpreted as the fraction of all units in the population that fail by time $t$. Since $F(t) = 0.992$ for this computer model, the fraction of this model that fail by time $t$ is 0.992. [III.E.1]

19. c; The exponential distribution is the only probability distribution to have a constant failure rate. For an exponential distribution with parameter $\lambda$, the hazard rate function $h(t) = \lambda$. [III.E.1]

From the following table, we can find the number of survivors up to time $t$ to find the solutions to questions 20–22.

| Upper bound (hours), $t_i$ | Number of failures, $x_i$ | Number of survivors, $n_i$ |
|---|---|---|
| 0 | 0 | 450 |
| 100 | 7 | 443 |
| 200 | 16 | 427 |
| 300 | 19 | 408 |
| 400 | 27 | 381 |

20. b; The estimated reliability at time $t = 200$ is

$$\hat{R}(t) = \frac{n_2}{N} = \frac{427}{450} = 0.9489.$$

[III.E.1]

21. a; The failure density is the probability density function defined as

$$\hat{f}(t) = \frac{n_3 - n_4}{(t_4 - t_3) \times N}.$$

Therefore,

$$\hat{f}(t) = \frac{408 - 381}{(400 - 300) \times 450} = 0.0006.$$

[III.E.1]

22. d; The instantaneous rate of failure is the hazard rate function $h(t)$ where

$$\hat{h}(t) = \hat{f}(t) / \hat{R}(t) = \frac{n_3 - n_4}{(t_4 - t_3) \times n_3} = \frac{408 - 381}{(400 - 300) \times 408} = 0.00066.$$

[III.E.1]

23. c; A series system has $n$ components connected end-to-end. If one component fails, the entire system fails. The reliability of a series system made up of $n$ components is

$$R_s(t) = R_1(t) \times R_2(t) \times \ldots \times R_n(t).$$

For this series system, the system reliability, therefore, is

$$R_s(t) = 0995^5 = 09752.$$

[III.E.2]

24. b; A parallel system is made up of components so that if one or more paths fail, the remaining path(s) are still able to perform properly. Therefore, the system fails when all units fail. The reliability of a parallel system is

$$R_s(t) = 1 - \left[ F_1(t) \times F_2(t) \times \ldots \times F_n(t) \right].$$

For this series system, the system reliability therefore, is

$$R_s(t) = 1 - \left[(1 - 0.995)\right]^5 = 0.999999$$

The reliability of the system is essentially 1. [III.E.2]

25. b; A parallel system is made up of $n$ components connected in parallel. Therefore, the system will fail only if all of the components or subsystems fail. [III.E.2]

26. a; A series system is made up of $n$ components connected end-to-end. Therefore, if one of the components fails, the entire system fails. The system reliability, therefore, is the product of the reliabilities of each subsystem. This means that the system reliability will be lower than the reliability of the subsystem with the lowest reliability. [III.E.2]

27. d; The machine has a $k$-out-of-$n$ system design where $k = 3$ and $n = 6$. The system reliability of a $k$-out-of-$n$ system is

$$R_s(t) = \Sigma_{i=k}^{n} \binom{n}{i} p^i (1-p)^{n-i}$$

where $p = 0.88$.

Therefore, the system reliability is

$$R_s(t) = \binom{6}{3}(0.88)^3(0.12)^3 + \binom{6}{4}(0.88)^4(0.12)^2 + \binom{6}{5}(0.88)^5(0.12)^1 + \binom{6}{6}(0.88)^6(0.12)^0$$

$$= 20(0.88)^3(0.12)^3 + 15(0.88)^4(0.12)^2 + 6(0.88)^5(0.12)^1 + 1(0.88)^6(0.12)^0$$

$$= 0.02355 + 0.1295 + 0.3799 + 0.4644$$

$$= 0.9975$$

[III.E.2]

28. c; The reliability of a standby system with $n$ standby components is

$$R_s(t) = e^{-\lambda t} \sum_{i=0}^{n} \frac{(\lambda t)^i}{i!}$$

In this case, the machine is a standby system where $n = 4$, $\lambda = 0.08$, and $t = 100$.

Therefore, the system reliability is

$$R_s(t) = e^{-(0.08)(100)} \sum_{i=0}^{4} \frac{(0.08 \times 100)^i}{i!} = e^{-8} \sum_{i=0}^{4} \frac{8^i}{i!}$$

$$= e^{-8} \left[ \frac{(8)^0}{0!} + \frac{(8)^1}{1!} + \frac{(8)^2}{2!} + \frac{(8)^3}{3!} \right] = 0.0424$$

[III.E.2]

29. d; The failure rate, $\lambda$, is the number of failures divided by the total test time. Therefore,

$$\lambda = \frac{28}{750 \times 5} = 0.0075$$

Note that the mean time to failure (MTTF) is

$$\frac{1}{\lambda} \approx 133,$$

assuming the life distribution is exponential. [III.E.2]

30. b; We are given that $R(400) = 0.645$. Recall that MTTF = 1/failure rate = $1/\lambda$. Since the reliability of the component is exponential, we have

$$R(t) = e^{-\lambda t} \rightarrow R(400) = e^{-\lambda(400)} = 0.645$$

$$\ln\left(e^{-\lambda(400)}\right) = \ln(0.645)$$

$$-400\lambda = \ln(0.645)$$

$$\lambda = \frac{\ln(0.645)}{-400}$$

$$\lambda = 0.0011$$

Therefore,

$$\text{MTTF} = \frac{1}{\lambda} = \frac{1}{0.0011} = 909.09 \approx 910 \text{ hours.}$$

[III.E.2]

31. a;

$$\text{MTTF} = 115 - \frac{1}{\lambda} = \frac{1}{\text{Failure rate}}.$$

This means that the failure rate, $\lambda$, is $\lambda = 1/115$. Since the reliability of the dishwasher has an exponential distribution, the probability that a randomly selected dishwasher survives past $t$ months is $R(t) = e^{-\lambda t}$. Therefore, the probability that a randomly selected dishwasher survives past 115 months is

$$R(115) = e^{-115/115} = e^{-1} = 0.3679.$$

[III.E.2]

32. b; Another interpretation of reliability is the fraction of all machines that survives past a time $t$. We can find this fraction using the reliability function $R(t) = e^{-\lambda t}$. Since

$$\text{MTTF} = 525, \ \lambda = \frac{1}{\text{MTTF}} = \frac{1}{525}, \ R(1000) = e^{-\left(\frac{1000}{525}\right)} = 0.1488.$$

Approximately 15% of the machines will survive past 1000 hours. [III.E.2]

33. d; The rechargeable battery is a repairable system (via recharging). Since the mean time between failures (MTBF) is five hours, the failure rate $\lambda = 1/5 = 0.2$. The probability that a battery fails by time $t$ describes the failure function $F(t) = 1 - R(t) = 1 - e^{-\lambda t}$.

Therefore,

$$F(6) = 1 - e^{-\frac{6}{5}} = 1 - 0.3012 = 0.6988$$

[III.E.2]

34. d; The mean time between failures (MTBF) is 900 hours. Therefore, the failure rate $\lambda = 1/900$. Assuming that the reliability of the component is exponential, the reliability at time $t = 500$ is defined as

$$R(500) = e^{-\lambda(500)} = e^{-500/900} = 0.5738$$

[III.E.2]

35. a; The reliability can be interpreted as the fraction of all components that survive past some time $t$. Therefore, $R(t) = e^{-\lambda t}$ and $R(MTTF) = e^{-\lambda(MTTF)}$. Since the failure rate for this component is $\lambda = 0.0008$,

$$MTTF = \frac{1}{\lambda} = \frac{1}{0.0008} = 1250$$

$$R(MTTF) = R(1250) = e^{-0.0008(1250)} = 0.3679$$

36.79% of all components survive past the mean time to failure of 1250 hours. [III.E.2]

36. c; The failure rate for this machine is $\lambda = 0.0008$, which means that the mean time between failures (MTBF) is

$$\frac{1}{\lambda} = \frac{1}{0.0008} = 1250 \text{ hours}$$

Since MTTR = 5 hours, the steady-state availability of the machine is

$$A = \frac{MTBF}{MTBF + MTTR} = \frac{1250}{1250 + 5} = 0.9960$$

[III.E.2]

37. c;

$$\lambda = \text{Failure rate} = \frac{\# \text{ failures}}{\text{Total test time}} = \frac{515}{600 \times 25} = 0.0343$$

Therefore,

$$MTBF = \frac{1}{\lambda} = \frac{1}{0.0343} = 29.1262 \approx 29$$

Since the mean time to repair the components is eight hours, the steady-state availability of the component is

$$A = \frac{MTBF}{MTBF + MTTR} = \frac{29.1262}{29.1262 + 8} = 0.7845$$

[III.E.2]

38. b; A corrective maintenance policy does not require any repairs or other preventive maintenance until a failure occurs. Therefore, this type of policy allows for the maximum run time between repairs. [III.E.2]

39. d; A preventive maintenance policy is recommended when the cost to repair the system after its failure is greater than the cost of maintaining the system before its failure and the failure rate is monotonically increasing. If the failure rate is decreasing, then the system is more likely to improve over time, and preventive actions would be a waste of resources. [III.E.2]

40. c; The second region of a bathtub curve is the constant failure rate region. This region is characterized by the inherent failure rate of the components of a product. [III.E.3]

41. c; The second region of the bathtub curve is characterized by a constant failure rate. The exponential distribution is the only probability distribution that has a constant failure rate; therefore, the exponential distribution is often used to model the second region of the bathtub curve. [III.E.3]

42. b; The third region of the bathtub curve, the wear-out region, is characterized by an increasing failure rate over time. This time-dependent failure rate is often modeled using the Weibull distribution. [III.E.3]

43. a; The main goal of an FMEA is to help a team identify and eliminate the negative effects of a potential failure before it occurs. [III.E.4]

44. c; An FMEA team should be composed of a cross-section of employees across several fields. At a minimum, the FMEA team should have a doctor, nurse, technician, engineer, and manager. An FMEA team should have members that are both technical and nontechnical to have many viewpoints represented during the process. [III.E.4]

45. d; An FMEA has several components: potential failure modes, the risk associated with each failure mode, corrective action plans for the most significant failure modes, and documentation on the system. [III.E.4]

46. c; The risk priority number (RPN) is determined by multiplying the three components of risk together: severity, occurrence, and detection. Therefore, $RPN = 8 \times 2 \times 6 = 96$. [III.E.4]

47. b; An FMECA is an assessment of risk that provides a prioritization of corrective action based on severity and occurrence of failure modes. [III.E.4]

# Part IV
## Product and Process Control

(72 questions)

Part IV
Questions

## QUESTIONS

1.  An employee works in an area of a facility where tools are painted. Which of the following would this employee find in the control plan for the process of painting tools?

    a.  The sample size and frequency of sampling to monitor the painting process

    b.  A detailed description of the painting process

    c.  A list of the machines used to paint the tools

    d.  All of the above

2.  Which of the following would you typically find in a reaction plan for a process?

    a.  Sampling plan

    b.  Control chart

    c.  Detailed methods to contain questionable products

    d.  Gage R&R study

3.  Why are work instructions an important component of process control?

    a.  They explain sampling procedures.

    b.  They identify bottlenecks in a process.

    c.  They help reduce process errors.

    d.  They help to manage quality costs.

4.  Why is it important to identify materials used in producing a product?

    a.  To help manufacturers reduce risk

    b.  To save money

    c.  To help ensure product reproducibility

    d.  None of the above

5.  Which of the following is one of the most effective methods of accounting for and tracking product materials?

    a.  Control charts

    b.  OC curves

    c.  Paper move tags

    d.  Radio frequency identification

6.  A food company is planning to release a new type of cookie. At what stage in the process should the company consider tracing the cookie's components?

    a.  Before the release of the cookie to the public

    b.  After any inquiries from customers

    c.  At the beginning of the cookie's development

    d.  Only when there is an increase in nonconforming cookies

7.  Keeping nonconforming products from being mixed with good/conforming products within a manufacturing plant is known as:

    a.  compliance.

    b.  material segregation.

    c.  material review.

    d.  defect classification.

8.  A recall due to a brake malfunction on an automobile was issued by a car company. How would the company classify this type of defect?

    a.  Minor defect

    b.  Major defect

    c.  Serious defect

    d.  Critical defect

9.  Customers have complained about the battery life for a new line of computers released. How would the computer company classify this type of product defect?

    a.  Minor defect

b.  Major defect

c.  Serious defect

d.  Critical defect

10. What purpose does the material review board of a company serve?

a.  Oversee the traceability of a product

b.  Develop sampling plans for product materials

c.  Identify the source of all product components

d.  Determine corrective action for nonconforming components

11. Acceptance sampling is most appropriate for inspecting products when:

a.  the product is complex.

b.  the fraction of nonconforming products is unknown.

c.  there are high inspection costs.

d.  the cost of making a wrong decision is high.

12. A disadvantage of sampling inspection compared to 100% inspection is:

a.  sampling has lower inspection costs.

b.  sampling is more time intensive than 100% inspection.

c.  sampling emphasizes that the supplier is concerned with quality.

d.  rejecting a lot that conforms to specification as a result of variability in sampling.

13. Which of the following tools is most appropriate when evaluating a sampling plan?

a.  Scatter plot

b.  Operating characteristic (OC) curve

c.  Process map

d.  Affinity diagram

14. A company requires a part on a small lot-by-lot basis. On which of the following probability distributions should the OC curve of the sampling plan be based?

a.  Hypergeometric distribution

b.  Binomial distribution

c.  Poisson distribution

d.  Normal distribution

15. A company is deciding between two competing sampling plans for a product they receive from a manufacturer. The diagram below displays the OC curves for these two sampling plans.

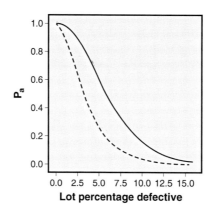

Compared to the solid line, the dashed OC curve:

a.  is better for the company.

b.  will accept lots with a higher probability.

c.  is better for the manufacturer.

d.  None of the above

16. Consider a sampling plan with $n = 45$ and $c = 2$. Given that the percentage nonconforming is 0.05 and a binomial distribution is appropriate, what is the probability of accepting the lot?

a.  0.3923

b.  0.6093

c.  0.6077

d.  0.3350

17. In acceptance sampling, what does the acronym "LTPD" mean?

a.  The quality level

b.  The poorest quality in an individual lot that should be accepted.

c.  The average quality of outgoing products

d.  The worst tolerable process average of a continuing series of lots.

18. Type I error in hypothesis testing corresponds to which of the following in acceptance sampling?

    a. Consumer's risk

    b. Producer's risk

19. Consider a sampling plan with $n = 45$ and $c = 2$. Given that the percentage nonconforming is 0.05 and a lot size assumed to be infinite, what is the average outgoing quality?

    a. 0.6077

    b. 0.3923

    c. 0.0304

    d. 0.9696

20. In an acceptance sampling plan, how does the probability of acceptance change as the sample size increases, assuming the acceptance number and lot size are held constant?

    a. $P_a$ increases.

    b. $P_a$ decreases.

    c. $P_a$ stays constant.

    d. Not enough information provided

21. Holding all else equal, which factor has the least effect on the OC curve?

    a. The lot size, $N$

    b. The sample size, $n$

    c. The acceptance number, $c$

    d. None of the above

22. In acceptance sampling, what is the AOQL?

    a. The minimum average outgoing quality limit

    b. The maximum average outgoing quality limit

    c. The average quality of outgoing products

    d. The poorest quality in an individual lot that should be accepted

23. At a particular factory, testing whether a lot obtained by a supplier is acceptable requires destructive testing. What type of sampling method is most appropriate?

    a.  Continuous sampling

    b.  Single sampling

    c.  Double sampling

    d.  Sequential sampling

24. What is a potential disadvantage of single sampling plans?

    a.  They do not use tightened inspection.

    b.  They are hard to administer in practice.

    c.  The sample size is adjustable for changes in incoming product quality.

    d.  All of the above

25. The attribute sampling plan for a specific product utilizes an acceptance value of 2 and rejection value of 5. The inspector discovers two defective items in the current sample. What is the next appropriate action?

    a.  Accept the lot since the number of defective items does not exceed the Ac value.

    b.  Accept the lot since the number of defective items is less than the Re value.

    c.  Reject the lot since the number of defective items is not less than the Ac value.

    d.  Draw another sample.

26. A double sampling plan is implemented with the following parameters:

$$n_1 = 50, \ c_1 = 1, \ r_1 = 4, \ n_2 = 75, \ c_2 = 3, \ r_2 = 6$$

What is the probability that a decision is made (to accept or reject the lot) on the first sample if the percentage nonconforming, $p$, is equal to 0.10?

    a.  0.2165

    b.  0.9221

    c.  0.7835

    d.  0.8614

27. A double sampling plan is implemented with the following parameters:

$$n_1 = 50, \; c_1 = 1, \; r_1 = 3, \; n_2 = 75, \; c_2 = 3, \; r_2 = 4$$

What is the average sample number for this sampling plan if the percentage nonconforming, $p$, is equal to 0.10?

a. 50

b. 125

c. 109

d. 67

28. When compared with sampling plans with equal protection, the average sample number of double sampling plans generally is:

a. smaller when the quality is poor.

b. larger when the quality is poor.

c. larger when the quality is near the indifference level ($p = 0.50$).

d. None of the above

29. Which of the following types of sampling is not allowed in ANSI/ASQ Z1.4-2003 (R2013)?

a. Single sampling

b. Sequential sampling

c. Double sampling

d. Multiple sampling

30. A lot size of 1500 is to be inspected using ANSI/ASQ Z1.4-2003 (R2013). The AQL is 0.40%. What is the required sample size for a single sampling plan (normal, level II inspection)?

a. 50

b. 80

c. 125

d. 200

31. A lot size of 500 is to be inspected using ANSI/ASQ Z1.4-2003 (R2013). The AQL is 0.65%. What are the required sample size, acceptance number, and rejection number for a single sampling plan (normal level II inspection)?

    a.  $n = 50$, Ac = 0, Re = 1

    b.  $n = 50$, Ac = 1, Re = 2

    c.  $n = 80$, Ac = 0, Re = 1

    d.  $n = 80$, Ac = 1, Re = 2

32. A lot of size 200 is to be inspected using ANSI/ASQ Z1.4-2003 (R2013). The AQL is 0.65%. What are the required sample sizes for a double sampling plan (normal, level II inspection)?

    a.  20, 40

    b.  13, 13

    c.  20, 20

    d.  32, 32

33. A lot of size 400 is to be inspected using ANSI/ASQ Z1.4-2003 (R2013). The AQL is 0.65%. For the first sample of a double sampling plan (normal, level II inspection), what are the acceptance and rejection numbers?

    a.  Ac = 1, Re = 4

    b.  Ac = 1, Re = 2

    c.  Ac = 0, Re = 3

    d.  None of the above

34. AOQL is used to build which kind of sampling plan?

    a.  Single sampling plan

    b.  Dodge-Romig sampling tables

    c.  Double sampling plan

    d.  Sequential sampling plans

35. An advantage of variables sampling plans compared to attribute sampling plans is that variables sampling plans:

    a.  require smaller sample sizes with equal protection compared to attribute sampling plans.

b.  are easier to implement.

c.  can monitor multiple quality characteristics at once.

d.  are less expensive to implement.

36. A lot of 100 items is submitted for inspection under ANSI/ASQ Z1.9-2003 (R2013), level II, normal inspection with AQL = 0.65%. Both upper and lower specification limits are specified for these items. What sample size is required for this sampling plan?

a.  5

b.  7

c.  10

d.  20

37. A lot of 20 items is submitted for inspection under ANSI/ASQ Z1.9-2003 (R2013), level II, normal inspection with AQL = 1.00%. The required sample size for this sampling plan is four. The results of the four measurements are: 51, 47, 45, 39. Does this lot meet the acceptance criteria? The upper and lower specification limits for this process are 52 and 37, respectively.

a.  Yes, since the total percentage nonconforming is less than the maximum allowable.

b.  No, since the total percentage nonconforming is less than the maximum allowable.

c.  Yes, since the total percentage nonconforming is more than the maximum allowable.

d.  No, since the total percentage nonconforming is more than the maximum allowable.

38. Which of the following parameters is not required to determine a sequential sampling plan?

a.  Producer's risk

b.  Consumer's risk

c.  Rejectable quality level

d.  AOQL

39. A sequential sampling plan has the following parameters:

$$\alpha = 0.01, \ AQL = 0.05, \ \beta = 0.15, \ RQL = 0.25$$

Which of the following statements about this sampling plan is true?

a. The plan has a 1% chance of rejecting a lot that is 25% defective.

b. The plan has a 1% chance of accepting a lot that is 5% defective.

c. The plan has a 15% chance of accepting a lot that is 25% defective.

d. The plan has a 15% chance of rejecting a lot that is 25% defective.

40. A sequential sampling plan has the following parameters:

$$\alpha = 0.01, \ AQL = 0.05, \ \beta = 0.15, \ RQL = 0.25$$

What is the equation for the reject line for this sampling plan?

a. $0.1281n - 1.0224$

b. $0.1281n - 2.4069$

c. $0.1281n + 2.4069$

d. None of the above

41. A sequential sampling plan has an accept line defined as: Accept line = $0.1043n - 1.2486$. For a sample size $n = 10$, what is the acceptance number?

a. 0

b. 1

c. 2

d. None of the above

42. A sequential sampling plan has a reject line defined as: Reject line = $0.1576n + 1.9397$. By what sample unit would you be able to reject a lot given this reject line?

a. 2

b. 3

c. 13

d. None of the above

43. Why is sampling integrity important?

a. To be able to accurately read an OC curve

b. To ensure that a product has not been contaminated during inspection

c. To have the most efficient process

d. To reduce the amount of sampling required

44. Which of the following is not a method used to maintain sample integrity?

    a. Uniquely identifying a batch of products

    b. Tracking changes made to a product

    c. Implementing 100% inspection

    d. Maintaining descriptive directions used to create a product

45. Which of the following is a result of dimensional inspection of a product?

    a. Improved quality of the product

    b. Conformity to customer aesthetic requirements

    c. Determination of a conforming or nonconforming product

    d. None of the above

46. Which of the following provides the most precise angular measurement?

    a. Protractor

    b. Bevel protractor

    c. Square

    d. Sine bar

47. The outside dimensions of a part are inspected for conformance to product specifications. Which of the following measuring tools is most appropriate for this measurement?

    a. Steel ruler

    b. Plug gage

    c. Snap gage

    d. Sine bar

48. A part was inspected using a go/no-go gage. The part did not mate with either end of the gage. Did the part pass the inspection?

    a. No, the part should be rejected.

    b. Yes, the part should be accepted.

    c. Not enough information provided

49. Which of the following methods is the most common for surface measurements?

    a. Reflectance meters

    b. Optical interference

    c. Pneumatics

    d. Stylus averaging

50. A key component of a part is round in shape. Which of the following measurement tools is most appropriate to measure this component?

    a. Ring gage

    b. Vernier calipers

    c. Precision spindle

    d. Dial indicator

51. The maximum tensile strength a particular part can withstand is an important quality characteristic of this part. Which of the following is most appropriate to test this quality characteristic?

    a. 100% inspection

    b. Screening inspection

    c. Coordinate measuring machine

    d. Nondestructive testing

52. Which of the following nondestructive tests can only be used on parts made of iron and steel?

    a. Liquid penetration testing

    b. Magnetic particle testing

    c. Eddy current testing

    d. Ultrasonic testing

53. Which of the following nondestructive tests can only be used on parts made of conductive materials?

    a. Liquid penetration testing

    b. Magnetic particle testing

    c. Eddy current testing

    d. Radiographic testing

54. Which of the following organizations maintains the standards of measurement in the United States?

   a. ISO

   b. ASQ

   c. NIST

   d. SI

55. Which of the following is critical in metrology?

   a. Physical artifacts

   b. Paper standards

   c. Definition of base units

   d. All of the above

56. How does NIST define the kilogram, the base unit of mass?

   a. As a physical artifact used for direct reference

   b. The amount of water required to fill a 36-ounce beaker

   c. Based on the weight of carbon molecules

   d. None of the above

57. Slight changes in temperature where parts are measured for conformance could lead to:

   a. systematic error in measurement.

   b. random error in measurement.

   c. operator error in measurement.

   d. type II error in measurement.

58. True/False. The most sensitive measuring equipment always leads to the most precise measurements.

   a. True

   b. False

59. To quantify a laboratory's measurement system to national standards, a company could use which of the following?

   a. Measurement assurance

b. Calibration

c. Traceability

d. Gage R&R study

60. Information on the contribution to error of technicians or a laboratory's procedures can typically be found in:

a. measurement calibration records.

b. measurement traceability protocols.

c. the material review board.

d. measurement assurance protocols.

61. The goal of equipment calibration is to maintain the system's:

a. accuracy.

b. precision.

c. sensitivity.

d. readability.

62. While analyzing repeated measurements of a quality characteristic, an employee notices that the values are consistently larger than the reference value. Which of the following has occurred in this measurement process?

a. Random error

b. Systematic error

c. Type I error

d. Type II error

63. Which of the following components of a measurement system contributes to its accuracy?

a. Repeatability

b. Reproducibility

c. Linearity

d. Random error

64. Which of the following does not contribute to variability in measurement system error?

a. Correlation

b. Linearity

c. Bias

d. Reproducibility

65. The length of a part should be 6.00 cm. A particular part is repeatedly measured six times, yielding the following measurements: 6.05, 5.94, 5.98, 6.01, 6.03, 5.97. What is the resulting bias for this part?

   a. 0.003

   b. 5.997

   c. −0.003

   d. 0.041

66. The lengths of three parts have the following reference values: 3.00 cm, 6.00 cm, 12.00 cm. Ten repeated measurements were taken for each type of part. The observed averages of these three samples were: 2.998, 5.843, 12.275. Which of the following statements is true?

   a. There is evidence of nonlinearity in this measurement system.

   b. There is evidence of stability issues in this measurement system.

   c. The measurement system is not reproducible.

   d. The measurement system is not repeatable.

67. The precision of a measurement system can be defined as:

   a. the difference between the recorded measurement and the target value of a quality characteristic.

   b. the variability present when the same part is measured multiple times under the same conditions.

   c. the ability to get the same degree of bias in a measurement over time.

   d. the ability to get the same degree of bias in a measurement for parts of different sizes.

68. In a gage R&R study, the variance associated with repeatability was found to be 0.8842 and the variance associated with reproducibility was found to be 0.2466. What is the variance associated with measurement error?

   a. 0.6376

   b. 1.4369

c.  1.1308

d.  Not enough information provided

69.  The ANOVA table below displays the results of a gage R&R study where two operators measured five parts three times each using the same gage.

| Source | df | SS | MS | F | p |
|---|---|---|---|---|---|
| Part | 4 | 44 | 11 | 12.69 | 0.015 |
| Operator | 1 | 0.033 | 0.033 | 0.04 | 0.854 |
| Part × Operator | 4 | 3.467 | 0.867 | 0.70 | 0.599 |
| Error | 20 | 24.667 | 1.233 | | |
| Total | 29 | 72.167 | | | |

Using this full model, what is the measurement error variability?

a.  0.867

b.  0

c.  1.233

d.  1.828

70.  Based on the results from the gage R&R study in the previous question (question 69), which of the following statements is true?

a.  There is a significant interaction between parts and operators.

b.  More operator training is necessary in this process.

c.  This is a capable process.

d.  None of the above

71.  Refer to the gage R&R study in question 69. Suppose that the upper and lower specification limits for the quality characteristic are 30 and 10, respectively. What is the precision-to-tolerance ratio for this process?

a.  0.333

b.  0.370

c.  0.406

d.  0.523

72. A gage R&R study was performed for a process using 10 parts, two operators, and three replicates. The *R*-chart below displays information about the gage capability. What conclusions can be drawn from this control chart?

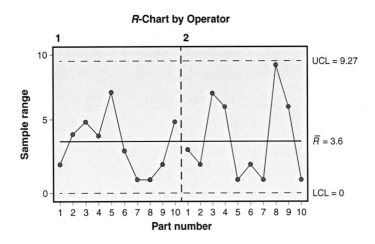

a. There are significant differences between operators.

b. The operators are consistent in their use of the gage.

c. The gage is not able to distinguish between parts.

d. The gage is able to distinguish between parts.

## SOLUTIONS

1. d; Control plans typically include the following: a description of the process, any equipment used in the process, reference drawing numbers, the process characteristic that is being controlled, how the process characteristic should be evaluated, the sampling plan, the method of control, and a reaction plan if the process goes out of control. [IV.A]

2. c; A reaction plan typically contains four elements: containment, diagnosis, verification, and disposition. The reaction plan should therefore include specific directions for the operators on how to contain products that are suspected of being nonconforming or out of spec. [IV.A]

3. c; Work instructions provide details of a process for those who operate the process. Providing detailed instructions helps eliminate errors by providing all required machine settings, setup instructions, and visual aids. [IV.A]

4. a; Knowing where materials come from also gives the manufacturers the ability to trace the product. This helps to reduce exposure to additional risks. [IV.B.1]

Part IV
Solutions

5. d; Radio frequency identification (RFID) is a common method used to identify and track materials using bar codes, scanners, and RFID receivers. RFID tags allow manufacturers to maintain detailed information about materials as well. [IV.B.1]

6. c; Product identification and traceability should begin when the process is being designed. Including traceability from the start will ensure adequate quality of the cookie and help reduce recall risks. [IV.B.1]

7. b; Material segregation ensures that nonconforming products are not mixed with conforming products. [IV.B.2]

8. d; A brake malfunction in a car could lead directly to a severe customer injury; therefore, this defect would be classified as critical. [IV.B.3]

9. b; The poor battery life of the computer reduces the usability of the product, but will not likely lead to an injury or significant economic loss. Therefore, the company would classify this as a major defect. [IV.B.3]

10. d; The material review board (MRB) determines the appropriate corrective action to take in the case that nonconforming components are discovered. It also determines any additional actions to take to prevent similar nonconformities in the future. [IV.B.4]

11. c; Acceptance sampling is most appropriate when the inspection costs are high or when destructive inspection is the only method of inspection. Acceptance sampling is also appropriate when the inspection of a product is monotonous and causes inspector fatigue, which could lead to an increase in inspection errors. [IV.C.1]

12. d; Sampling inspection has several advantages as it saves time and energy compared to 100% inspection. However, there is variability inherent in sampling. Therefore, there are chances of making type I and type II errors: rejecting lots that conform to the quality specifications or accepting lots that do not conform to quality specifications. [IV.C.1]

13. b; An operating characteristic (OC) curve displays the probability of accepting lots at varying levels of percentage nonconforming. It provides a simple, graphical way to evaluate a sampling plan. Scatter plots are appropriate to analyze the relationship between two variables. A process map is used to help understand the steps of a process. Affinity diagrams are useful as a planning tool to help organize ideas generated by a group. [IV.C.1]

14. a; Because the products are received on a lot-by-lot basis and are not part of a continuous process, the OC curve should be based on the hypergeometric

distribution. This OC curve is called a type A OC curve. Type B OC curves are used to evaluate a sampling plan for a continuous process or for a process that has a large lot size. Type B OC curves are developed using the binomial or Poisson distributions. [IV.C.1]

15. a; The dashed OC curve is better for the consumer. As the percentage nonconforming increases, the probability of accepting the lot decreases much faster compared to the other OC curve. This means that the company will accept fewer unacceptable lots from the producer. [IV.C.1]

16. c; The probability of acceptance is defined as

$$P_a = P(d \le c) = \sum_{d=0}^{c} \binom{n}{d} p^d (1-p)^{n-d}$$

Note that

$$\binom{n}{d} = \frac{n!}{d!(n-d)!}$$

In this example, $n = 45$, $c = 2$, and $p = 0.05$. So,

$$P_a = \sum_{d=0}^{2} \binom{45}{d}(0.05)^d (0.95)^{n-d} = 0.6077$$

[IV.C.1]

17. b; LTPD is the *lot tolerance percent defective*, expressed in percentage defective. It is the worst quality level in an individual lot that should be accepted when submitted for acceptance sampling. Consequently, the LTPD has a low probability of acceptance. [IV.C.1]

18. b; A type I error in hypothesis testing is the probability of rejecting the null hypothesis when in fact the null hypothesis is true. Therefore, type I error corresponds to the producer's risk in acceptance sampling: the probability that a lot is rejected when in fact the lot is within the acceptable quality level. [IV.C.1]

19. c; Assuming an infinite lot size, the *average outgoing quality* (AOQ) can be calculated as AOQ = $P_a p$. In this sampling plan,

$$P_a = \sum_{d=0}^{2} \binom{45}{d}(0.05)^d (0.95)^{n-d} = 0.6077$$

Therefore, AOQ = (0.6077)(0.05) = 0.0304. [IV.C.1]

20. b; As the sample size increases, the probability of acceptance decreases. Consider, for example, an infinite lot size, an acceptance number $c = 1$, and fraction nonconforming $p = 0.05$. For various sample sizes $n$, we have the following probability of acceptance:

| Sample size ($n$) | $P_a$ |
|---|---|
| 2 | 0.9975 |
| 5 | 0.9774 |
| 10 | 0.9139 |
| 20 | 0.7358 |

[IV.C.1]

21. a; The lot size, $N$, has the smallest effect on the OC curve compared to the acceptance number $c$ and the sample size $n$. [IV.C.1]

22. b; AOQL stands for the average outgoing quality limit and is the maximum average outgoing quality level for a given sampling plan. The AOQL is the highest value on an AOQ curve. [IV.C.1]

23. d; Sequential sampling is advantageous when testing samples is costly or destructive. This type of sampling plan greatly reduces the sample sizes necessary for acceptance sampling. [IV.C.2]

24. a; The sample size of a single sampling plan does not change, regardless of changes in incoming product quality levels. Therefore, reduced or tightened inspection is not implemented with single sampling plans, which typically reduces sampling costs. [IV.C.2]

25. a; When using a double sampling plan, after you take the first sample you will either accept the lot, reject the lot, or draw another sample. If the number of defective items in the first sample, $d_1$, is less than or equal to the acceptance number, then you accept the lot. If $d_1$ is greater than the rejection number value, then you reject the lot. If $d_1$ is more than the acceptance number but less than the rejection number, then you draw another sample. In this case, $d_1 = 2 = Ac$. Therefore, the lot is accepted, and another sample does not need to be drawn. [IV.C.2]

26. c; Let $D_1$ denote the probability that the lot is accepted or rejected on the first sample. Let $d_1$ denote the number of defects found in the first sample. We will accept the lot if there are one or fewer defects noted in the first sample. We

will reject the lot if there are four or more defects in the first sample. (Another sample will be drawn if two or three defects are found in the first sample.) Therefore,

$$P(D_1) = P(d_1 \le 1) + P(d_1 \ge 4) = 1 - P(d_1 = 2) - P(d_1 = 3)$$

$$= 1 - \binom{50}{2}(0.10)^2(0.90)^{48} - \binom{50}{3}(0.10)^3(0.90)^{47}$$

$$= 1 - 0.0779 - 0.1386 = 0.7835$$

[IV.C.2]

27. d; Let $P_2$ denote the probability of requiring a second sample. From the previous problem (question 26), the probability of only drawing one sample is 0.7835. Therefore, the probability of requiring a second sample $P_2 = 1 - 0.7835 = 0.2165$. For a double sampling plan, the average sample number is defined as ASN = $n_1 + n_2P_2 = 50 + 75 \times 0.2165 = 66.24$ or 67. [IV.C.2]

28. a; When the quality of the lots is very good or very poor, the average sample size will generally be smaller compared with other sampling plans with equal protection. This is because the probability of making a decision on the first sample will tend to be higher, and thus fewer second samples are required. When the quality of the lots is near the indifference level ($p = 0.50$), the average sample number of double sampling plans is rarely larger. [IV.C.2]

29. b; ANSI/ASQ Z1.4-2003 (R2013) allows for single sampling, double sampling, and multiple sampling. [IV.C.2]

30. c; Given that the lot size is 1500, the sample size code letter from the ANSI/ASQ Z1.4-2003 (R2013) sampling tables (ANSI/ASQ Z1.4-2003 [R2013] Table 1) for normal, level II sampling is K. Regardless of the AQL level, the required sample size is $n = 125$ (from ANSI/ASQ Z1.4-2003 [R2013] Table II-A). [IV.C.2]

31. b; Given that the lot size is 500, the sample size code letter from the ANSI/ASQ Z1.4-2003 (R2013) sampling tables for normal, level II sampling is H. Using ANSI/ASQ Z1.4-2003 (R2013) Table II-A, the required sample size is 50. Using the AQL of 0.65%, the downward arrow points to the sampling plan for code letter J. Therefore, the acceptance number is 1 and the rejection number is 2. [IV.C.2]

32. c; Given that the lot size is 200, the sample size code letter from the ANSI/ASQ Z1.4-2003 (R2013) sampling tables for normal, level II sampling is G (Table 1). Using ANSI/ASQ Z1.4-2003 (R2013) Table III-A, Double Sampling Plans for Normal Inspection, and the same size code letter G, the sample size required is 20 for both the first and second sample regardless of the AQL. [IV.C.2]

33. d; Given that the lot size is 400, the sample size code letter from the ANSI/ASQ Z1.4-2003 (R2013) sampling tables for normal, level II sampling is H (Table 1). Using ANSI/ASQ Z1.4-2003 (R2013) Table III-A, Double Sampling Plans for Normal Inspection, the same size code letter H, and AQL = 0.65%, the downward arrow points to the sampling plan for code letter J. Therefore, the acceptance number for the first sample is 0 and the rejection number for the first sample is 2. [IV.C.2]

34. b; Dodge-Romig tables use the AOQL and LTPD for plan selection. The plans are designed to minimize average total inspection. [IV.C.2]

35. a; Variables control charts offer equal protection compared to an attribute sampling plan with a much smaller sample size. However, they are generally more expensive to implement and are much harder to administer. They also can only monitor one quality characteristic at a time. [IV.C.2]

36. c; ANSI/ASQ Z1.9-2003 Table A-2 gives sample size code letter F. From ANSI/ASQ Z1.9-2003 Table B-3, this code letter corresponds to a sample size of 10, regardless of the AQL level. [IV.C.2]

37. d; Note that USL = 52, LSL = 37. From the provided sample data, $\bar{x}$ = 45.5, $s$ = 5.00. Using this information, we can calculate the two quality indices for the sampling plan:

$$Q_u = \frac{USL - \bar{x}}{s} = \frac{52 - 45.5}{5} = 1.30$$

and

$$Q_L = \frac{\bar{x} - LSL}{s} = \frac{45.5 - 37}{5} = 1.70$$

From ANSI/ASQ Z1.9-2003 Table A-2, the sample size code letter for this situation is C. Using Table B-3 (since we have double specification limits) and the AQL level of 1.00%, the maximum allowable percentage nonconformity (M) is $M$ = 1.49%. We can now use Table B-5 to estimate the lot percentage nonconforming. The percentage above the specification limit with $n$ = 4 and $Q_U$ = 1.30 is 6.67%. The percentage below the specification limit with $n$ = 4 and $Q_L$ = 1.70 is 0.00%. The total percentage nonconforming is 6.67% + 0.00% = 6.67%. Since the percentage nonconforming is greater than M, the maximum allowable percentage nonconforming, we conclude that the lot is not acceptable. [IV.C.2]

38. d; To determine a sequential sampling plan, the producer's risk ($\alpha$), the consumer's risk ($\beta$), the acceptable quality level (AQL = $p_1$), and the rejectable or limited quality level (RQL = $p_2$) are required. [IV.C.2]

39. c; $\beta = 15\%$ is the consumer's risk and is the probability of accepting a lot that does not meet the quality levels. RQL = 25% is the rejectable (or unacceptable) quality level. Therefore, the plan has a 15% chance of accepting a lot that is 25% nonconforming. [IV.C.2]

40. c; $\alpha = 0.01$, AQL $= p_1 = 0.05$, $\beta = 0.15$, RQL $= p_2 = 0.25$.

    The reject zone line is defined by: Reject line $= sn + h_2$

    The accept zone line is defined by: Accept line $= sn - h_1$

$$a = \log\left(\frac{1-\beta}{\alpha}\right) = \log\left(\frac{1-0.15}{0.01}\right) = 4.4427$$

$$b = \log\left(\frac{1-\alpha}{\beta}\right) = \log\left(\frac{1-0.01}{0.15}\right) = 1.8871$$

$$h_1 = \frac{b}{\log\left(\frac{p_2(1-p_1)}{p_1(1-p_2)}\right)} = \frac{1.8871}{\log\left(\frac{0.25(1-0.05)}{0.05(1-0.25)}\right)} = 1.0224$$

$$h_2 = \frac{a}{\log\left(\frac{p_2(1-p_1)}{p_1(1-p_2)}\right)} = \frac{4.4427}{\log\left(\frac{0.25(1-0.05)}{0.05(1-0.25)}\right)} = 2.4069$$

$$s = \frac{\log\left((1-p_1)/(1-p_2)\right)}{\log\left(\frac{p_2(1-p_1)}{p_1(1-p_2)}\right)} = \frac{\log\left(\frac{1-0.05}{1-0.25}\right)}{\log\left(\frac{0.25(1-0.05)}{0.05(1-0.25)}\right)} = 0.1281$$

    Therefore, the reject line is defined as: Reject line $= sn + h_2 = 0.1281n + 2.4069$ [IV.C.2]

41. d; Given: $n = 10$ and Accept line $= 0.1043n - 1.2486$. The acceptance number can be found by plugging $n = 10$ into the accept line equation:

    Accept line $= (0.1043)(10) - 1.2486 = -0.2056$.

    Since the acceptance number is negative, acceptance is not possible for this sample size. Additional samples must be taken. [IV.C.2]

42. b; Given: Reject line $= 0.1576n + 1.9397$. Rejection of a lot is not possible when the rejection number is greater than the sample number. Therefore, rejection of the lot will be possible when the rejection number is less than the sample number. We can find this sample number since we require

$$0.1576n + 1.9397 < n$$

$$1.9397 < (1 - 0.1576)n$$

$$n > \frac{1.9397}{1 - 0.1576}$$

$$n > 2.303$$

Therefore, rejection of a lot is possible on the third sample unit. [IV.C.2]

43. b; Sample integrity is necessary to ensure that a product has not been misused or contaminated and to ensure that sampling is accurate to the entire lot of products. [IV.C.3]

44. c; To maintain sample integrity, you can use batch control (which includes documenting the steps used to create the product, giving unique identification numbers to each batch produced, and maintaining a log listing the amount of each material inserted into the batch), change control (which involves classifying and tracking changes made to a product), and configuration control (an extension of change control). [IV.C.3]

45. c; Dimensional inspection involves measurement of a product to determine whether the product meets required specifications. Inspecting a product to determine if it meets the specifications, however, does not determine its quality. The quality of the product will depend on the engineering design and how it was manufactured. [IV.D.1]

46. d; A sine bar is more precise for measuring angles as compared to protractors, bevel protractors, or squares. [IV.D.1]

47. c; Gages are used to determine conformance (or nonconformance) of a part's dimensions to specifications. Specifically, snap or ring gages are used to check outside dimensions; plug gages are used to check inside dimensions. [IV.D.1]

48. a; A part passes inspection with a go/no-go gage if the part mates with the go end and does not mate with the no-go end. Since this part did not mate with either end, it did not pass the "go" inspection. Therefore, the part should be rejected. [IV.D.1]

49. d; Using a stylus to measure an average electrical signal is the most common method of surface measurement because it is fast, repeatable, interpretable, and relatively inexpensive. [IV.D.1]

50. c; Precision spindle instruments are used for roundness measurements. Calipers are used for linear measurements, ring gages are used to assess specification conformance of outside dimensions, and dial comparators are used to check operations (for example, verify alignments). [IV.D.1]

51. d; Measuring the maximum tensile strength of a part would be destructive to the part. Therefore, screening inspection or 100% inspection is not appropriate; nondestructive testing is required. [IV.D.2]

52. b; Magnetic particle testing is used on parts that can be magnetized; therefore, magnetic particle testing can be done only on parts made of iron, steel, or allied materials. [IV.D.2]

53. c; Eddy current testing applies an AC current through a coil near the surface of the part under inspection; therefore, only parts made of conducting materials can be tested with eddy current testing. [IV.D.2]

54. c; The National Institute of Standards and Technology (NIST) maintains the standards of measurement in the United States. [IV.E]

55. d; All three of these areas must be taken into account in metrology. Physical artifacts must be manufactured with high precision (for example, gage blocks) in order to be used as masters for reference. Paper standards include the published documents that contain the specifications or accepted methods for taking measurements. Definition of base units is critical as they form a reference from which all other units are derived. [IV.E]

56. a; The kilogram is the only base unit that is defined in terms of a physical artifact, which is made of a platinum-iridium alloy and protected by the International Bureau of Weights and Measures in Paris. A duplicate is also protected by NIST in the United States. [IV.E]

57. b; Errors in measurement are classified as *random* errors (accidental fluctuations that can not be predicted) or *systematic* errors (for example, operator error or calibration error). Ambient changes like slight temperature changes in a laboratory are classified as random error. [IV.E]

58. b; Sensitivity is associated with the equipment and is defined as the least perceptible change in dimension detected by the measuring tool and shown by the indicator. Precision is associated with the actual measuring process; therefore, the most sensitive instrument may not always lead to the most precise results. [IV.E]

59. c; Traceability is intended to quantify a laboratory's measurement uncertainty compared to national standards. [IV.E]

60. d; Measurement assurance protocols provide details on the accuracy of a measuring instrument as well as the contribution to measurement error of technicians, the laboratory environment, and a laboratory's procedures. [IV.E]

61. a; The aim of calibration is to maintain a measuring system's accuracy. [IV.E]

62. b; In measurement systems analysis, there are two types of errors: *systematic* error and *random* error. Systematic error can be caused by humans, imprecise measuring devices, or poor manufacturing methods. It will remain relatively constant over repeated measurements. Random error is inherent fluctuations in the measurement system. Type I and type II errors are found in hypothesis testing (type I error occurs when a true null hypothesis is rejected; type II error occurs when a false null hypothesis is not rejected). [IV.F]

63. c; The accuracy of a measurement system consists of gage bias, linearity, and stability. Repeatability and reproducibility describe the precision of the measurement system. [IV.F]

64. a; Measurement system error variability can be attributed to gage bias, stability, linearity, repeatability, reproducibility, and accuracy. Correlation measures the linear relationship between two quantitative variables. [IV.F]

65. c; *Bias* is defined as the observed average minus the reference value. In this example, the reference value is 6.00 cm. The observed average is

$$\bar{x} = \frac{6.05 + 5.94 + 5.98 + 6.01 + 6.03 + 5.97}{6} = 5.997.$$

Therefore, Bias = 5.997 – 6.00 = –0.003. [IV.F]

66. a; Consider the bias for each of the three types of parts. Recall that

Bias = Observed average – Reference value

| Part | 1 | 2 | 3 |
|---|---|---|---|
| Reference value | 3.00 | 6.00 | 12.00 |
| Observed average | 2.998 | 5.843 | 12.275 |
| Bias | –0.002 | –0.157 | 0.275 |

*Linearity* measures how changes in the size of the part being measured affect the bias of the measurement system. In this example, the bias worsens as the length of the part increases, indicating evidence of nonlinearity in the measurement system. *Stability* is a measure of how well the measurement system performs over time. *Repeatability* is the variability of the test instrument when used to measure the *same* part. *Reproducibility* is the variability due to different operators or setups of the measurement system measuring the *same* part. [IV.F]

67. b; *Precision* is defined as the variability encountered when the same part is repeatedly measured using the same measurement system under identical conditions. Precision is made up of repeatability and reproducibility. *Accuracy* refers to the relationship between the results from a measurement system and the target or reference value. [IV.F]

68. c; Note that in this gage R&R study,

$$\sigma^2_{\text{Reproducibility}} = 0.8842 \text{ and } \sigma^2_{\text{Repeatability}} = 0.2466.$$

$$\sigma^2_{\text{Measurement error}} = \sigma^2_{\text{Reproducibility}} + \sigma^2_{\text{Repeatability}} = 0.8842 + 0.2466 = 1.1308.$$

[IV.F]

69. c; The variance components can be found as follows:

Operators:

$$\hat{\sigma}^2_O = \frac{\text{MS}_O - \text{MS}_{PO}}{pr} = \frac{0.033 - 0.867}{5 \times 3} = 0$$

(Set to 0 since this variance component is negative)

Part × Operator:

$$\hat{\sigma}^2_{PO} = \frac{\text{MS}_{PO} - \text{MS}_E}{r} = \frac{0.867 - 1.233}{3} = 0$$

(Set to 0 since this variance component is negative)

Parts:

$$\hat{\sigma}^2_P = \frac{\text{MS}_P - \text{MS}_{PO}}{or} = \frac{11 - 0.033}{2 \times 3} = 1.828$$

Error:

$$\hat{\sigma}^2_e = \text{MS}_e = 1.233$$

$$\hat{\sigma}^2_{\text{Reproducibility}} = \hat{\sigma}^2_{PO} + \hat{\sigma}^2_O = 0$$

$$\hat{\sigma}^2_{\text{Repeatability}} = \hat{\sigma}^2_e = 1.233$$

$$\hat{\sigma}^2_{\text{Measurement error}} = \hat{\sigma}^2_{\text{Gage}} = \hat{\sigma}^2_{\text{Reproducibility}} + \hat{\sigma}^2_{\text{Repeatability}} = 0 + 1.233 = 1.233$$

[IV.F]

70. d; Based on the *p*-values from the ANOVA table from question 69, there is not a significant operator effect, indicating that the operators are performing well and no additional training is needed. Also from the ANOVA table, there is not a significant interaction between part and operator. However, by looking at the percentage contribution of the gage R&R variation to the total variability, we see that the variability associated with repeatability is quite large. This indicates that the gage is not capable and the process needs to be investigated to reduce the variation associated with repeatability. [IV.F]

| Source | Variance component | % contribution |
|---|---|---|
| Total gage R&R | 1.233 | 40.28 |
| Repeatability | 1.233 | 40.28 |
| Reproducibility | 0 | 0 |
| Operator | 0 | 0 |
| Operator × Part | 0 | 0 |
| Part-to-part | 1.828 | 59.72 |
| **Total variation** | **3.061** | **100** |

71. a; From question 69, we have that

$$\hat{\sigma}^2_{Gage} = \hat{\sigma}^2_{Measurement\ error} = 1.233$$

Therefore,

$$PTR = \frac{6\hat{\sigma}_{Gage}}{USL - LSL} = \frac{6 \times \sqrt{1.233}}{30 - 10} = 0.333$$

[IV.F]

72. b; An *R* chart provides information about special causes of variation related to the gage R&R study. In this example, no points plot outside the control limits, indicating that the operators behave similarly and that there are no special causes of variation (for example, operator fatigue or operator training issues). [IV.F]

# Part V
## Continuous Improvement

### (57 Questions)

## QUESTIONS

1. A team at a cell phone manufacturer would like to reduce the number of defects in the manufacture of their cell phones. They identify potential defects of the cell phone. What quality control tool is most appropriate to determine the most frequent defects?

    a. Pareto chart

    b. Scatter diagram

    c. Flowchart

    d. Control chart

2. A team at a radiology clinic in a hospital wants to improve patient flow in their clinic. Before making changes to their process, the team discusses potential causes of disruptions in the patient flow. Which quality control tool will best help this team organize this information?

    a. Flowchart

    b. Scatter diagram

    c. Cause-and-effect diagram

    d. Check sheet

3. The team in the radiology clinic has collected data on patient visit times. The team suspects that the data are heavily skewed. Which of the following quality control tools would be most appropriate to confirm the team's suspicions?

    a. Histogram

    b. Scatter diagram

    c. Pareto chart

    d. Control chart

4. A team at a manufacturing facility is in the beginning stages of a performance improvement project to reduce the number of defects in a toy they produce. The team would like to collect data in order to decide the best opportunities for improvement. Which quality control tool is most appropriate to organize this data?

   a. Flowchart

   b. Check sheet

   c. Scatter diagram

   d. Histogram

5. A team at a bank wants to improve the time it takes to process a loan application. In order to identify any bottlenecks in the process or targets for improvement, which quality control tool is most appropriate to use?

   a. Pareto chart

   b. Check sheet

   c. Scatter diagram

   d. Flowchart

6. The bank has implemented changes to their loan application process and would like to monitor their improvements to ensure they are sustained. Which of the following quality control tools would best help this effort?

   a. Control chart

   b. Flowchart

   c. Check sheet

   d. Scatter diagram

7. A team suspects that two variables are related. Which of the following quality control tools will help them determine this?

   a. Histogram

   b. Flowchart

   c. Pareto chart

   d. Scatter diagram

8. A project team in a company comprises a large group of employees from different departments. The project has many complex components that depend

on the progress of the various departments. Which of the following tools would help this team maintain a schedule for their project?

a.  Prioritization matrix

b.  Activity network diagram

c.  Tree diagram

d.  Interrelationship digraph

9.  A clinic in a hospital is beginning a project to improve patient wait times. The project team is determining critical-to-quality factors. Which tool would be most appropriate to use?

a.  Value stream map

b.  Cause-and-effect diagram

c.  PVC diagram

d.  SIPOC diagram

10.  A national print and copy company is considering changing the layout of their stores across the country to better serve their customers. The store is in the early phase of implementing their rollout plan for these changes. Which of the following tools would help the company evaluate their rollout plan to ensure there are minimal disruptions?

a.  Matrix diagram

b.  Process decision program chart

c.  Activity network diagram

d.  Prioritization matrix

11.  An accident has recently occurred in a factory's shipping area. A team was put together to analyze potential actions that could lead to similar accidents. The goal is for the team to help determine the risk associated with these actions and to prevent future accidents from occurring. Which quality tool would help this team visualize this scenario?

a.  Fault tree

b.  Affinity diagram

c.  Matrix diagram

d.  Process decision program chart

12. A management team has a brainstorming meeting to identify opportunities to improve communication within their department. Which quality tool will best help them organize all the ideas generated by the team?

    a. Tree diagram

    b. Matrix diagram

    c. Affinity diagram

    d. Activity network diagram

13. Which of the following tools is common in quality function deployment and used to map customer requirements with technical specifications of a product?

    a. Prioritization matrix

    b. Activity network diagram

    c. Matrix diagram

    d. Interrelationship digraph

14. A medical team meets to discuss potential cause-and-effect relationships of actions that could lead to unfavorable outcomes during a patient surgical operation. The team consists of nurses, doctors, physician assistants, and technologists. Which of the following tools would best help this team visualize and hopefully identify factors that cause unfavorable outcomes?

    a. Affinity diagram

    b. Interrelationship digraph

    c. Prioritization matrix

    d. Activity network diagram

15. A cell phone manufacturer is developing a new cell phone. The research and development team has been given several required components of the phone, but have not decided on a design plan. Which of the following quality tools would help this team explore potential design plans for the new cell phone?

    a. Fault tree

    b. Prioritization matrix

    c. Concept fan

    d. Process decision program chart

16. The research and development team have now proposed several designs for the new cell phone. The team is now considering which of the designs to pursue to build a prototype. Which of the following tools would best help the team reach a decision on which of the designs to use?

    a. Prioritization matrix

    b. Affinity diagram

    c. Interrelationship digraph

    d. Process decision program chart

17. A team in the packing department of a shoe company noticed some inefficiencies in their packing process. The team first reduced the amount of walking employees had to do by moving the labeling station next to the packing station. The team continued to make incremental changes to their process, each of which led to a small improvement of the process. Which improvement technique has this team made use of?

    a. Six Sigma

    b. Total quality management (TQM)

    c. Kaizen

    d. Plan–do–check–act (PDCA)

18. In the PDCA cycle, in which stage of this improvement method does a team define the problem and develop an action plan?

    a. P

    b. D

    c. C

    d. A

19. Which of the following continuous improvement methods focuses on a business's customers, quality built into the work culture, and strong leadership involvement in quality efforts?

    a. Kaizen

    b. TQM

    c. PDCA

    d. Theory of constraints (TOC)

Part V
Questions

20. A quality team in a semiconductor factory, using the PDCA cycle, has proposed a change to their process. They have implemented the change and are currently analyzing the results. In which step of the PDCA cycle is this quality team?

    a. P

    b. D

    c. C

    d. A

21. What is the primary goal of kaizen improvement?

    a. Eliminate waste in a process.

    b. Reduce the number of defects produced in a process.

    c. Redesign a process to make large improvements in quality.

    d. Make small, incremental changes to a process.

22. A product in a shipping company goes through many subprocesses as it is shipped to the customer. Customers were experiencing long wait times until their product arrived. The shipping company examined their current process and discovered that packing the product was the slowest subprocess. The company decided to focus their improvement efforts on this subprocess. Which of the following improvement methods does this scenario describe?

    a. TOC

    b. TQM

    c. Kaizen

    d. PDCA

23. What is one of the primary goals of Six Sigma as a continuous improvement method?

    a. Eliminate waste in a process.

    b. Reduce the number of defects produced in a process.

    c. Redesign a process to make large improvements in quality.

    d. Make small, incremental changes to a process.

24. What is the primary strength of theory of constraints?

    a. Incremental changes to a process can lead to great improvements.

b.  A system can not improve by focusing improvements solely on individual processes.

c.  Team-based projects are more effective than individual-based projects.

d.  A data-driven improvement strategy is necessary for process improvement.

25. In Six Sigma, what value of sigma ($\sigma$), the standard deviation of a process, is used to account for typical shifts or drifts from the mean?

a.  $\pm 2\sigma$

b.  $\pm 6\sigma$

c.  $\pm 3\sigma$

d.  $\pm 1.5\sigma$

26. A restaurant with a particularly large kitchen and lots of empty space had long delays preparing and serving patrons. After careful planning, the restaurant completely redesigned their kitchen and ordering procedures, and immediately saw a vast decrease in serving times. They also noticed an increase in customers after this change. Which of the following improvement methods does this scenario describe?

a.  PDCA

b.  TQM

c.  Reengineering

d.  Kaizen

27. What value of $C_p$ is associated with a six sigma–quality level process?

a.  1.33

b.  1.5

c.  2.0

d.  2.5

28. Which of the following methods is the most effective way to implement Six Sigma in an organization?

a.  Start a Six Sigma program.

b.  Develop a Six Sigma infrastructure.

c.  Roll out Six Sigma methods on a project-by-project basis.

d.  None of the above

29. Which of the following tools is typically used first in a lean system?

    a. 5S

    b. Kanban

    c. Value stream map

    d. Visual control

30. A restaurant is analyzing their current work flow. Employees in the restaurant must walk back and forth throughout the kitchen to retrieve various cooking tools during preparation of a meal. How might the restaurant classify this action?

    a. Waiting

    b. Excess motion

    c. Excess movement of material

    d. Excess processing

31. The restaurant is also examining their front-of-house operations. They found that there is frequently a long line of customers standing by the chicken counter while staff turn over tables. What kind of waste is occurring at the front of house at this restaurant?

    a. Waiting

    b. Excess movement of material

    c. Defect correction

    d. Excess motion

32. After creating a value stream map of a process, on which steps in the process should a quality team focus their efforts?

    a. Value-added activities

    b. Standardized work

    c. Non-value-added activities

    d. All of the above

33. What is the primary goal of 5S?

    a. To radically change a process

b. To make slow, incremental changes to a process

c. To organize the workplace environment

d. To reduce defects produced in a process

34. A toy company paints a certain toy white by default. The toys are then painted other colors as requested by customers. As what type of waste might a quality team classify this action?

a. Defect correction

b. Excess motion

c. Excess processing

d. Excess production

35. What is the main benefit of implementing a kanban system?

a. The weakest step in a chain of processes is improved.

b. There is less inventory and a smoother flow of supplies.

c. The workplace is better organized.

d. Products are not processed until a customer places an order.

36. A deli has newly instituted a few changes to their work area. The workers now have a schedule for cleaning their workstations, have standardized practices, and have created designated locations for all their equipment. What improvement method has this deli employed?

a. Kanban

b. Visual control

c. Define, measure, analyze, improve, control (DMAIC)

d. 5S

37. A factory uses an illuminated indicator light when a certain process is in progress. This is an example of:

a. waste.

b. standardized work.

c. visual control.

d. kanban.

38. In a convenience store, items are stacked in front of a card that lists details on the product, including the location of additional boxes in their storage room as well as a number to call to reorder. What type of system has this convenience store implemented?

    a. Kaizen

    b. 5S

    c. TQM

    d. Kanban

39. To complete a process, parts must travel through four departments located in different areas of a manufacturing facility. As what type of waste would a quality team at the facility classify this process?

    a. Excess movement of material

    b. Defect correction

    c. Excess processing

    d. Excess motion

40. A manufacturing facility has painted arrows on the floor to show the flow of products through the facility. Which lean tool has this facility implemented?

    a. Kanban

    b. Visual control

    c. 5S

    d. Kaizen

41. The principle that each process should be done the same way, every time, by every employee is called:

    a. kanban

    b. 5S

    c. standardized work

    d. pull system

42. Which of the following lean tools measures the time from the last good part of one type to the first good part of the next?

    a. Takt time

    b. Single-minute exchange of die (SMED)

c. Cycle time

d. 5S

43. What is the difference between cycle time and takt time?

    a. Cycle time incorporates data from suppliers; takt time does not.

    b. Takt time is based on customer demand; cycle time measures the time to complete an activity.

    c. Takt time measures the time to complete an activity; cycle time incorporates customer demand.

    d. There is no difference; they both measure the same time.

44. A shoe company routinely makes more components than are needed when assembling their product. As what type of waste might this company classify this action?

    a. Inventory

    b. Overproduction

    c. Excess movement of material

    d. Excess processing

45. A university has released a document detailing all the required actions instructors should take when proctoring an exam. All instructors across the university are expected to follow these directions. What tool has the university implemented?

    a. Standardized work

    b. 5S

    c. Visual control

    d. Value stream map

46. A company has received an order for 550 items that they need to produce in an eight-hour workday. In seconds, what is the takt time for this product?

    a. 0.87 seconds

    b. 68.75 seconds

    c. 52.36 seconds

    d. None of the above

Part V
Questions

47. A caterer had a lunch order for a group of 50 people and had two hours to complete the order. However, after two hours, the caterer was only able to complete 45 lunches. Which of the following must be true?

    a. Cycle time ≤ Takt time

    b. Cycle time > Takt time

    c. Cycle time = Takt time

    d. None of the above

48. A radiation clinic treats patients with different types of cancer. The position of each patient on the table is different depending on the type of cancer. Therefore, after one patient is treated, another patient, requiring a different setup than the previous patient, arrives. Which lean tool would best help a quality team in this clinic?

    a. Cycle time

    b. 5S

    c. SMED

    d. Kanban

49. A supplier has received an order from one of their customers. They must complete an order of 750 items in a daytime shift that is 10 hours long. The cycle time for this process is 50 seconds. Without any changes in their current production, will the supplier be able to meet the customer's demands?

    a. No, since cycle time ≤ takt time.

    b. Yes, since cycle time ≤ takt time.

    c. No, since cycle time > takt time.

    d. Yes, since cycle time > takt time.

50. What is one of the most common causes of failures in problem solving?

    a. Poor definition of the problem

    b. Multifunctional teams

    c. Selecting projects that require the least amount of effort

    d. The project charter

51. During the correction phase of the corrective action cycle, which of the following is instrumental in success?

    a. A clear problem statement

    b. Team meetings

    c. Creativity

    d. Cause-and-effect diagram

52. A team in a food production plant has recently instituted changes to one of their bottling processes. What should the team do to avoid the process backsliding?

    a. Identify key metrics in the process to monitor

    b. Specify who performs each task in the process

    c. Institute process certification for operators

    d. All of the above

53. In which phase of the corrective action cycle does a team seek to continuously improve the performance of a process by holding regular reviews of the process?

    a. Problem identification

    b. Correction

    c. Recurrence control

    d. Effectiveness assessment

54. Which of the following is another name for poka-yoke?

    a. Waste

    b. Error-proofing

    c. Orderliness

    d. Pull system

55. A food company produces cookie dough. All a customer must do is slice the cookie dough and bake it in their oven for approximately eight minutes. The company's cookie dough recipe was developed so that the cookie quality is not vastly affected by differences in ovens, elevation, or other environmental conditions. This cookie dough is an example of:

    a. poka-yoke.

    b. reengineering.

   c. robust design.

   d. kaizen.

56. A printer that will only run when the paper trays are closed is an example of which of the following concepts?

   a. Robust design

   b. Poka-yoke

   c. Lean process

   d. Kaizen

57. Before the next step in a process, a sorting machine is used to remove components that are above the upper specification limit. What principle of error-proofing is implemented in this process?

   a. Elimination

   b. Replacement

   c. Facilitation

   d. Detection

   e. Mitigation

## SOLUTIONS

1. a; Pareto charts are used to identify the most frequent issues in a process. The chart displays the "80/20 rule"—approximately 20% of factors (defects) account for approximately 80% of potential issues. Scatter diagrams graphically compare the relationship between two continuous variables, flowcharts provide a graphical representation of a process, and control charts are used to identify out-of-control behavior in a process. [V.A]

2. c; Cause-and-effect diagrams (also called *fishbone* or *Ishikawa* diagrams) are used to identify all major and minor factors that contribute to a problem. These diagrams can help the team identify the best opportunities for improvement in patient flow in the clinic. [V.A]

3. a; Histograms are a graphical representation of the frequency of occurrences of some event. They provide a visual depiction of the shape and spread of the data and can therefore help the team decide whether the data are skewed, symmetric, bimodal, and so on. Scatter diagrams are used to depict the relationship between two continuous variables. Pareto charts are graphical tools used to identify the most frequent events. [V.A]

4.  b; Check sheets are useful tools for summarizing counts of events, for example, the count of different types of defects. The data collected from a check sheet can then be graphically represented with a Pareto chart to identify the most frequent defects. Scatter diagrams graphically depict the relationship between two continuous variables, and histograms provide a graphical representation of the distribution for a continuous variable. [V.A]

5.  d; Flowcharts are a graphical representation of a process and can help identify areas for improvement (like a bottleneck). Pareto charts are used to identify the most common defects, check sheets are used to tally occurrences of events, and scatter diagrams are used to graphically depict the relationship between two continuous variables. [V.A]

6.  a; Control charts can be used to monitor a quality characteristic, in this case the time until the loan applications are processed. A time that plots beyond the control limits will indicate that a special cause has occurred. This alert will help the team correct the problem and to maintain their improvements. [V.A]

7.  d; Scatter diagrams are used to graphically depict the relationship (if there is one) between two continuous variables. Histograms are graphical tools used to depict the distribution of one continuous variable. [V.A]

8.  b; Activity network diagrams help to organize complex schedules or sequences of events. These diagrams, in particular, can help with time scheduling. Because this project involves a large group of people and is dependent on the work of different departments, an activity network diagram would help keep all the team members aware of the project schedule to avoid bottlenecks during the project. [V.B]

9.  d; A SIPOC diagram is a process map that contains information on the suppliers, inputs, outputs, and customers of a process. The diagram helps to capture the voice of the customer and the critical-to-quality factors. [V.B]

10. b; A process decision program chart (PDPC) would help this company assess their national rollout plan at a high level since they are at the beginning of their implementation plan. These charts help to determine potential disruptions to a process plan so that the company can prepare for any necessary contingency plans. [V.B]

11. a; Fault trees provide a visualization of hierarchical relationships of events that lead to some failure (or other undesirable final outcome). The team here wishes to determine other potential actions that can lead to a similar accident in the factory. The fault tree would help the team identify and communicate other potential causes of the accident. The fault tree would also provide a means to quantify the risks of these potential causes. [V.B]

Part V
Solutions

12. c; Affinity diagrams are used to help a group of people organize or summarize facts, opinions, or ideas. Often, these types of diagrams are built using sticky notes that are grouped into common themes or categories. [V.B]

13. c; Matrix diagrams are used to display qualitative relationships between two sets of characteristics or factors. Therefore, these diagrams are common in quality function deployment because they clearly display the relationships between customer requirements and a product's technical specifications. [V.B]

14. b; Interrelationship digraphs provide a means to identify sequential or cause-and-effect relationships of a problem or situation, in this case an unfavorable outcome in the operating room. Affinity diagrams are used to organize general thoughts and ideas about a topic and are more appropriate for grouping related ideas rather than discovering causal relationships. Prioritization matrices provide a formal method for comparing decisions or ideas before making a final decision. Activity network diagrams help to organize events for time schedule planning. [V.B]

15. c; A concept fan is a type of tree diagram that allows a team to explore alternate concepts that achieve the same goals or requirements. Fault trees are also tree diagrams but provide information on the hierarchical events that lead to an unfavorable outcome or failure in a process. Prioritization matrices provide a formal method for comparing decisions or ideas before making a final decision. Process decision program charts (PDPCs) help to evaluate a process implementation plan at a high level. [V.B]

16. a; Prioritization matrices are useful in the decision phase since they allow us to make relative comparisons of different ideas or concepts with consistent criteria. The R&D team has developed several competing designs and can use a prioritization matrix to fairly compare the designs to help them make a final decision. [V.B]

17. c; The packing team has made several minor changes to their process, each of which led to a small improvement. This describes kaizen, a methodology that encourages employees to make incremental changes continually to improve a process. Each change may not make a large improvement, but does help employees. [V.C]

18. a; In the *plan* phase of the plan–do–check–act (PDCA) cycle, the quality team decides on a potential change to the process. In the *do* phase, the team performs the proposed change, in the *check* step, the team analyzes the results of the change, and in the *act* phase, the team decides either to accept the change or not, depending on whether the change was successful or not. [V.C]

19. b; Total quality management (TQM) is an organization-wide quality program that focuses on customers' involvement in determining quality, employees' obligation to quality, and strong leadership from upper management in quality improvement efforts. Kaizen is a method of continuous improvement that makes incremental changes to a process. PDCA, also called the Shewhart or Deming (PDSA) cycle, is a methodology for a performance improvement project, and theory of constraints (TOC) is a problem-solving methodology that focuses on the weakest part of a process. [V.C]

20. c; The quality team has already implemented the proposed change and are analyzing the results. This describes the *check* step of the PDCA cycle. In this step, the quality team should carefully analyze the results of their change to determine whether the change was successful or not. In the *act* step, the team will make a decision on whether to keep the change, and then repeat the cycle. [V.C]

21. d; The primary goal of kaizen is for employees to make continual, incremental changes to a process to achieve small improvements. Lean focuses on eliminating waste in a process, one of the goals of Six Sigma is to reduce defects, and reengineering involves redesigning a process to see large improvements in quality of a product. [V.C]

22. a; Theory of constraints focuses on the weakest process in a string of processes to improve the overall system. In the shipping company, products can not be delivered more quickly unless the bottleneck in packing is improved. [V.C]

23. b; One of the primary goals of Six Sigma is to reduce the number of defects produced in a process. Lean focuses on eliminating waste in a process, reengineering involves redesigning a process to see large improvements, and kaizen is continuous, incremental improvements to a process. [V.C]

24. b; TOC focuses on the weakest link in a chain of processes—therefore, it's a systems approach to process improvement. Focusing on an individual process in a chain of many will not provide the best result. [V.C]

25. d; The sigma quality level includes a $\pm 1.5\sigma$ value to account for typical drifts from the mean. [V.C]

26. c; Reengineering a process involves a complete and radical redesign of a procedure. In this case, the restaurant has completely redesigned their kitchen and ordering procedure in order to achieve large improvements in their serving time and sales—an example of reengineering. [V.C]

27. c; Recall that the process capability index $C_p$ is defined as

$$C_p = \frac{USL - LSL}{6\sigma}.$$

A six sigma–quality level process has a $C_p$ value of 2.0 (and a $C_{pk}$ value of 1.5). [V.C]

28. b; One of the drawbacks of a Six Sigma program is that they often lack buy-in across the entire organization because they focus on the tools only. Therefore, results tend to be very limited. A Six Sigma infrastructure provides employees not just with the tools, but also with the problem-solving methods for specific projects identified by management. [V.C]

29. c; The goal of a lean system is to eliminate waste from a process. The first step is to identify opportunities for improvement, which can be found using a value stream map. Value stream maps are a visual representation of all the steps in a process, including information about timing. Value stream maps also identify the value-added and non-value-added activities in a process. [V.D]

30. b; The employees walk more than they should to retrieve supplies. This is an example of waste—specifically, that of excess motion. A redesign of the kitchen or a new layout that moves the cooking tools closer to where they are required could help reduce the excess walking and shorten the time it takes to prepare the meal. [V.D]

31. a; The customers are waiting to be seated at the restaurant due to the long setup/turnover times of the tables. The restaurant may want to cross-train their employees or introduce standardized work to help reduce the setup time and therefore the customer waiting time. [V.D]

32. c; Non-value-added activities are any steps in a process that are unneeded in the process. Improvement projects will have the largest impact on these non-value-added steps in a process. [V.D]

33. c; 5S stands for five Japanese words that detail ways to better organize a workplace. NIST defines these in English as sort, set in order, shine, standardize, and sustain. Note that reengineering involves radically changing a process, kaizen implements slow, incremental changes to a process, and one of the goals of Six Sigma is to reduce the number of defective items. [V.D]

34. c; This is an example of waste due to excess processing. The toys are all painted one color (white), then may be repainted per customer demands. The company may want to implement a new procedure for painting the toys so that they are not painted until a customer has requested their desired color. This would eliminate the need to paint the toys more than once. [V.D]

35. b; A kanban system provides visual cues to help ease restocking efforts. As a result, there is often less inventory and a better flow of supplies. Theory of constraints (TOC) focuses on improving the weakest step in a chain of processes. 5S is used to organize a workplace. A pull system means that the steps in a

process are completed only when triggered by a previous action, for example, a customer order. [V.D]

36. d; 5S stands for five words adopted from Japanese that detail ways to better organize a workplace. These include arranging things properly, orderliness, cleanliness, cleanup, and discipline. By incorporating a system for cleaning, developing standardized practices, and maintaining order with their equipment, this deli is implementing the five S's. [V.D]

37. c; A visible signal, like a light, is an example of visual control. The light is a cue to the employees that an action is being performed. These visuals help make employees more aware of their surroundings, which can help create a safer or more efficient workplace. [V.D]

38. d; A kanban system uses visual cues to help resupply efforts. When a bin of a particular item at the convenience store is emptied, the card alerts the convenience store employee where to find additional supplies, or how to order more. [V.D]

39. a; This is an example of waste due to excess movement of material. A layout change in the facility that groups together all assembly processes for a given product could reduce the distance the components must travel. Note that excess motion refers to more motion than necessary that employees or operators must make to complete an activity. [V.D]

40. b; This is an example of visual control. Arrows on the floor of the facility provide employees quick, visual cues on the flow of traffic. This will help movement in the facility and reduce errors and/or accidents. [V.D]

41. c; Standardized work means that every step or activity should be done the same way. Standardized work helps to reduce process variation and provides a more consistent product or service. [V.D]

42. b; Single-minute exchange of die (SMED) is a method used to reduce changeover times of machines. The goal of using SMED is to reduce the time required to switch a machine or assembly to a different product. [V.D]

43. b; Cycle time is the time it takes to complete an activity or process step. Takt time is based on customer demand and is defined as

    Takt time = (Time available) ÷ (Units required)

    The takt time therefore is the average time a process takes to complete one item out of the customer demand. [V.D]

44. b; This is an example of waste due to overproduction. This form of waste involves making more of a product than is necessary. In this case, the shoe company

consistently makes more components than they need, which is a waste of their resources and time. The company should adjust their production of this component. [V.D]

45. a; The university has implemented standardized work. All instructors are expected to follow the exam instructions the same way, every time. The goal of standardizing the exam procedure should help the process run smoother and make it more efficient across the university. [V.D]

46. c; Takt time is defined as

$$\text{Takt time} = (\text{Time available}) \div (\text{Units required})$$

The time available in seconds is $8 \times 60 \times 60 = 28{,}800$ seconds. Therefore,

$$\text{Takt time} = 28{,}800 \div 550 = 52.36 \text{ seconds}$$

Therefore, the company must average one item every 52.36 seconds. [V.D]

47. b; The takt time for the caterer (in minutes) is $2 \times 60 \div 50 = 2.4$ minutes. Therefore, the caterer needs to average a lunch every 2.4 minutes to meet customer demand. Since the caterer was only able to finish 45 lunches in the two hours, the cycle time must have been greater than the takt time. [V.D]

48. c; Single-minute exchange of die is a method used to reduce changeover times. Although initially introduced in a factory setting, the same methodology could apply in the radiation clinic as there are required changeover times for the different types of patients. [V.D]

49. c; The takt time for this system is $10 \times 60 \times 60 \div 750 = 48$ seconds. The supplier must average one item every 48 seconds. Because the cycle time (50 seconds) is greater than the takt time, the supplier is unlikely to meet the customer demand without any adjustments to their production. [V.D]

50. a; One of the most frequent sources of failure in problem solving is having a poor definition of the problem. Problem statements should be clear, focused, use facts and not judgment, and establish what is known, unknown, and needs to be done. [V.E]

51. c; In phase one of the corrective action cycle, the problem is identified and a clear problem statement is required. In phase two, the current process is analyzed and the root cause is identified, frequently through cause-and-effect diagrams. In the next phase, correction, an optimal solution is developed to solve the problem. In this phase, creativity is essential to best solve the problem. [V.E]

52. d; The recurrence control phase of the corrective action cycle involves the standardization of the solution to the problem. In this phase, the team should

identify the important variables that need to be kept under control. In addition, the team specifies all the details about the process—who does what, when, and how. Operator certification is also essential so that everyone knows their responsibilities at all times. [V.E]

53. d; In the problem identification phase, the team identifies areas for improvement and develops a clear problem statement. In the correction phase, the team develops feasible solutions to the problem and recommends the best choice to implement. In the recurrence control phase, the team standardizes the solution to ensure that the problem does not reoccur and prevent backsliding. Finally, in the effectiveness assessment phase, the team continues monitoring the process to identify additional opportunities for improvement. [V.E]

54. b; Poka-yoke comes from Japan and is also known as error-proofing. It is a method of preventive action—a technique used to prevent errors from occurring. Note that waste is also known as *muda*, and orderliness is one of the five S's (*seiton*). [V.F]

55. c; Because the quality of the cookie is not greatly affected by differing use conditions, this is an example of robust design. A robust design prevents or reduces variation in quality under various use conditions. [V.F]

56. b; Poka-yoke, or error-proofing, is used for error prevention. The printer not being allowed to run if a paper tray is open prevents paper jams or other possible errors. [V.F]

57. d; Detection is the principle that a defect or error is caught before it moves to the next step in the process. In this scenario, the sorting machine removes components that exceed the upper specification limit before moving to the next step in the process. [V.F]

# Part VI
## Quantitative Methods and Tools

(120 questions)

## QUESTIONS

1. A project is being conducted in a hospital clinic. Which of the following is not considered discrete data?

    a. Patient weight

    b. Result of a pass/fail medical test

    c. Errors in a medical record

    d. Number of patient visits

2. A project is being conducted in a manufacturing facility. Which of the following is not considered continuous data?

    a. The length of a component

    b. Fill volume of a container

    c. Number of nonconforming components

    d. Time required for testing

3. The color of a car is on which measurement scale?

    a. Nominal

    b. Ordinal

    c. Interval

    d. Ratio

4. A person's height in feet is on which measurement scale?

    a. Nominal

    b. Ordinal

    c. Interval

    d. Ratio

5. The rating of a service from poor to excellent is on which measurement scale?

    a.  Nominal

    b.  Ordinal

    c.  Interval

    d.  Ratio

6. A research team is doing a study on students at a college and would like to ensure that their sample has all four levels of students: freshmen, sophomores, juniors, and seniors. What sampling method is most appropriate for this study?

    a.  Double sampling

    b.  Stratified sampling

    c.  Simple random sampling

    d.  Multiple sampling

7. The waiting times in minutes for eight customers at a bank are: 5, 8, 12, 3, 2, 7, 6, 5. What are the mean and median for this sample of waiting times?

    a.  $\bar{X}$ = 5.5 minutes, M = 6 minutes

    b.  $\bar{X}$ = 6 minutes, M = 5 minutes

    c.  $\bar{X}$ = 6 minutes, M = 5.5 minutes

    d.  $\bar{X}$ = 6 minutes, M = 6 minutes

8. The lengths in inches for a sample of seven components are: 3.2, 3.1, 3.4, 3.1, 3.2, 3.3, 3.2. What is the standard deviation for this sample?

    a.  $s$ = 0.1069 in

    b.  $s$ = 0.0114 in

    c.  $s$ = 0.0098 in

    d.  $s$ = 0.0989 in

9. The median of a population is much larger than the population mean. What can you say about the shape of the population distribution?

    a.  The distribution is symmetric.

    b.  The distribution is right-skewed.

    c.  The distribution is left-skewed.

    d.  None of the above

10. A population has an exponential distribution. One hundred samples of size 40 are randomly collected and the 100 sample means are calculated. What is the approximate distribution of these sample averages?

   a.  Binomial

   b.  Normal

   c.  Uniform

   d.  Poisson

11. What is the formula for the population variance?

   a.  $\dfrac{\Sigma_{i=1}^{N}\left(x_i - \mu\right)}{N}$

   b.  $\dfrac{\Sigma_{i=1}^{n}\left(x_i - \bar{x}\right)^2}{n-1}$

   c.  $\dfrac{\Sigma_{i=1}^{N}\left(x_i - \mu\right)^2}{N}$

   d.  $\dfrac{\Sigma_{i=1}^{N}\left(x_i - \mu\right)^2}{N-1}$

12. A team would like to compare waiting times of customers by day of the week. Which of the following would be the most appropriate tool to use?

   a.  Histograms

   b.  Box plots

   c.  Scatter plots

   d.  Probability plots

13. Which of the following descriptive statistics is not typically found in a box plot?

   a.  Minimum

   b.  Maximum

   c.  Mean

   d.  Median

14. Which of the following is an advantage of a stem-and-leaf plot compared to a histogram?

   a.  Stem-and-leaf plots contain more information than a histogram.

b.  Stem-and-leaf plots provide a depiction of the shape of the data.

c.  Stem-and-leaf plots provide a time reference.

d.  None of the above

15. A team measured the time to failure of 20 components. They plotted the data in a normal probability plot, shown below. What conclusions can be drawn from this plot?

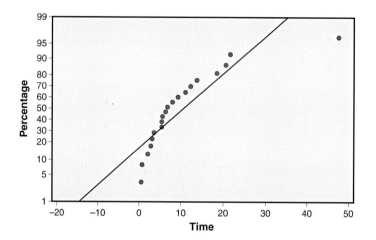

a.  The normal distribution is not a reasonable model for the time to failure.

b.  The Weibull distribution is a reasonable model for the time to failure.

c.  The normal distribution is a reasonable model for the time to failure.

d.  Not enough information provided to draw conclusions

16. The temperature of coffee is an important characteristic in a restaurant. The temperature of 15 randomly selected cups of coffee is measured and the average temperature is found to be 168 °F. Which term best describes this average temperature?

a.  Population

b.  Sample

c.  Parameter

d.  Statistic

17. A characteristic of a population is called a:

a.  Sample

b.  Statistic

    c. Parameter

    d. Probability

18. The contingency table below describes the relationship between the number of nonconforming components produced and time of day.

| Time | Conforming parts | Nonconforming parts | Totals |
|---|---|---|---|
| Day | 94 | 5 | 99 |
| Evening | 87 | 10 | 97 |
| Overnight | 65 | 23 | 88 |
| Totals | 246 | 38 | 284 |

Given that a part is made overnight, what is the probability it is nonconforming?

    a. 0.08

    b. 0.61

    c. 0.43

    d. 0.26

19. The probability of a part being defective is 0.02. What is the probability it is not defective?

    a. 0.88

    b. 0.98

    c. 1.08

    d. 2%

20. The probability that event A occurs is 0.72. The probability that event B occurs is 0.03. What is the probability that events A and B both occur?

    a. 0.0216

    b. 0.75

    c. 0.69

    d  Not enough information provided

21. If the probability that event A occurs is 0.40, the probability that event B occurs is 0.13, and A and B are mutually exclusive events, what is the probability that events A and B both occur?

    a. 0

    b. 0.052

    c. 0.53

    d. 1.27

22. The time between arrivals at a store has an exponential distribution with mean five minutes. What is the probability that the time between arrivals is less than three minutes?

    a. 0.9999

    b. 0

    c. 0.5488

    d. 0.4512

23. X has a normal distribution with mean 15 and standard deviation 2. What is the probability that X is greater than 18?

    a. 0.0668

    b. 0.8554

    c. 0.9332

    d. 0.1446

24. Which of the following probability distributions is not symmetric?

    a. Normal

    b. $t$

    c. Uniform

    d. None of the above

25. A bottling company's filling process has a normal distribution with mean 24.01 oz and standard deviation 0.025 oz. If the specifications for the process are 24 ± .08 oz, what proportion of bottles is overfilled?

    a. 0.99488

    b. 0.00256

  c. 0.99744

  d. 0.00016

26. Compared to the standard normal distribution, the Student's *t*-distribution:

  a. has a larger mean.

  b. is more skewed to the right.

  c. is bimodal.

  d. has heavier tails.

27. The number of nonconformities per inspection unit in a factory occurs at a rate of five per day. Using the most appropriate probability distribution, what is the probability there will be at least two nonconforming units in one day?

  a. 0.0404

  b. 0.2627

  c. 0.9596

  d. 0.8000

28. A sample of 10 products is selected from a small, isolated lot without replacement. The lot is known to contain 5% defective products. Which distribution is most appropriate to determine the probability of selecting at least one defective item in the sample?

  a. Hypergeometric

  b. Binomial

  c. Poisson

  d. Normal

29. Fifteen invoices are randomly selected from a batch at a company. It is believed that 10% of all invoices have an error. What is the probability that exactly four out of the 15 invoices have an error?

  a. 0.0428

  b. 0.9873

  c. 0.0127

  d. 1.0421

30. Suppose the number of errors in an invoice at a company has the probability mass function (written in table form) shown below. What is the expected number of errors in a randomly selected invoice?

| Number of errors X | 0 | 1 | 2 | 3 | 4 |
|---|---|---|---|---|---|
| Probability | 0.86 | 0.06 | 0.04 | 0.03 | 0.01 |

    a. 0.27

    b. 0.5771

    c. 0.7597

    d. 0

31. A population has a distribution with mean 24 and standard deviation 5.5. According to the central limit theorem, what is the mean of the distribution of the sample means for random samples of size 32?

    a. 24/5.5

    b. 24/32

    c. 24

    d. $24/\sqrt{32}$

32. A bottling company's filling process has a normal distribution with mean 24 oz and standard deviation 0.05 oz. What is the probability that a sample of 16 randomly selected bottles will have an average volume more than 24.04 oz?

    a. 0.9993

    b. 0.0007

    c. 0.2119

    d. 0

33. A sample of size 16 is drawn from a population that follows a normal distribution with mean 58 and variance 64. What is the standard error of the sample mean?

    a. 8

    b. 2

    c. 16

    d. 4

34. The 95% confidence interval for the proportion of filing errors in a business is (0.02, 0.12). What conclusions can be drawn from this confidence interval?

    a. There is a 95% chance that the population proportion $p$ is between 0.02 and 0.12.

    b. The probability that the confidence interval contains the population proportion $p$ is 0 or 1.

    c. We are 95% confident that the confidence interval will contain the population proportion $p$.

    d. b and c

    e. All of the above

35. A team would like to estimate the average length of a component. A random sample of 50 components had a sample mean of 11.75 mm. Which of the following terms is used to describe this value?

    a. Point estimate

    b. Parameter

    c. Probability

    d. Standard error

36. The tensile strength of 15 units of cement was tested. The sample mean tensile strength was 4.3 MPa and sample standard deviation was 0.51 MPa. Find a 99% confidence interval for the true mean tensile strength of the cement.

    a. (4.018, 4.582)

    b. (2.782, 5.818)

    c. (3.961, 4.639)

    d. (3.908, 4.692)

37. A team would like to estimate the true average tensile strength of cement. They would like to obtain an estimate within 0.15 MPa of the true average tensile strength with 95% confidence. Based on prior information, it is assumed that $\sigma = 0.50$ MPa. What sample size is required to meet these requirements?

    a. 43

    b. 42

    c. 6

    d. 7

38. The voltage of a power supply is of interest to a team. Voltage is assumed to be normally distributed. The voltages of seven randomly selected observations are: 10.37, 11.50, 9.80, 10.65, 11.95, 10.15, 9.52. Find the 95% confidence interval on the population variance of voltage.

    a.  (9.745, 11.380)

    b.  (0.570, 1.946)

    c.  (0.378, 4.419)

    d.  (0.324, 3.788)

39. A bottling factory claims that the volume of soda filled in bottles is 18 oz. You want to test whether the true mean volume of soda is different than 18 oz. The volume of a random sample of 24 bottles had a mean of 17.98 oz with a standard deviation of 0.03 oz. Using a significance level of 5%, what is the appropriate test statistic for this hypothesis test?

    a.  3.266

    b.  2.069

    c.  −3.266

    d.  −0.667

40. Suppose that the $p$-value of the hypothesis test posed in the previous question (question 39) is 0.003. What conclusions can be made (use significance level 5%)?

    a.  There is not sufficient evidence to conclude that the mean volume is different than 18 oz.

    b.  There is sufficient evidence to conclude that the mean volume is different than 18 oz.

    c.  18 would be contained in a 95% confidence interval of the population mean.

    d.  None of the above

41. Speed bumps were installed in a neighborhood to slow traffic. After installation, the speeds after the last speed bump of a random sample of 20 cars were recorded. The mean speed was 24.50 mph and the standard deviation was 2.3 mph. The team wanted to determine if the average speed is less than 25 mph. What are the appropriate hypotheses for this hypothesis test?

    a.  $H_0: \mu = 25$ versus $H_a: \mu \neq 25$

b. $H_0: \mu > 25$ versus $H_a: \mu = 25$

c. $H_0: \mu = 25$ versus $H_a: \mu < 25$

d. $H_0: \mu = 25$ versus $H_a: \mu > 25$

42. A team investigated the number of patient falls in a hospital. 56 patients were randomly selected. Out of the 56 patients, there were six recorded patient falls. The hospital wanted to determine whether the proportion of patient falls was more than 10%. At the 5% significance level, what is your conclusion to this hypothesis test?

   a. Reject $H_0$, conclude that the proportion of patient falls equals 0.10.

   b. Reject $H_0$, conclude that the proportion of patient falls is more than 0.10.

   c. Do not reject $H_0$, conclude that the proportion of patient falls equals 0.10.

   d. Do not reject $H_0$, conclude that the proportion of patient falls is more than 0.10.

43. Two methods for filling a bottle are being compared at a factory. The 90% confidence interval for the difference in volume for two independent random samples of the filling methods was found to be (−0.091, −0.049). Based on this confidence interval, is there evidence that the two filling methods are different?

   a. Yes, since 0 is not in the confidence interval.

   b. Yes, since 0 is in the confidence interval.

   c. No, since 0 is not in the confidence interval.

   d. No, since 0 is in the confidence interval.

44. An improvement project was done at a factory to decrease packaging time. The following data were collected before and after the improvement project:

   Before: Sample mean = 3.52, Sample variance = 2.34, Sample size = 28

   After: Sample mean = 2.10, Sample variance = 2.04, Sample size = 25

   A hypothesis test was performed with $H_0: \mu_{Before} - \mu_{After} = 0$ versus $H_a: \mu_{Before} - \mu_{After} > 0$. What is the critical value for this hypothesis test (Use $\alpha = 0.01$)?

   a. −2.403

   b. 2.403

   c. 2.678

   d. 2.576

45. Consider the scenario in the previous problem (question 44). The project team would like to determine whether the variance of packaging time has changed at the 10% significance level. What is the test statistic for the appropriate hypothesis test?

    a.  1.071

    b.  3.494

    c.  1.930

    d.  1.147

46. Two machines produce the same parts. A random sample of 1250 parts from machine 1 has 28 that are nonconforming, and a random sample of 1175 parts from machine 2 has 18 that are nonconforming. Find the 90% confidence interval for the difference between the proportions of nonconforming parts from machine 1 and 2.

    a.  (−0.002, 0.016)

    b.  (−0.004, 0.018)

    c.  (0, 0.016)

    d.  (0.006, 0.008)

47. A hypothesis test is performed at the 10% significance level. The power of the test is 0.80, or 80%. What is the type II error for this hypothesis test?

    a.  0.90

    b.  0.10

    c.  0.80

    d.  0.20

48. When the null hypothesis is not rejected when in fact the null hypothesis is false, what type of error has been made?

    a.  Sampling error

    b.  Type I error

    c.  Type II error

    d.  No error has been made

49. A team would like to compare the proportion of defective widgets produced by two machines. What distribution does the test statistic for this hypothesis test follow?

    a. Normal

    b. $t$

    c. Poisson

    d. Uniform

50. The heart rates of 12 individuals were measured using two different pieces of equipment. A team would like to compare the measured heart rates of the two pieces of equipment. Which hypothesis test would be most appropriate?

    a. Paired $t$-test

    b. Two-sample $t$-test

    c. Two-sample $p$-test

    d. Goodness-of-fit test

51. The length of five components was measured by two inspectors (data shown below). Assuming the data follow a normal distribution, what is the test statistic for the appropriate hypothesis test for this scenario? Use $\alpha = 0.01$.

| Component | 1 | 2 | 3 | 4 | 5 |
|---|---|---|---|---|---|
| Inspector A | 10.2 | 9.8 | 10.1 | 10.3 | 10.4 |
| Inspector B | 10.0 | 9.9 | 10.3 | 10.0 | 10.3 |

    a. 2.576

    b. 0.65

    c. 0.45

    d. 4.604

52. A team at a hospital did a project on medication errors. A random sample of medication errors yielded the following results.

| Type of error | Number of errors |
|---|---|
| Incorrect dose | 32 |
| Wrong dose | 28 |
| Incorrect form | 45 |
| Wrong amount | 35 |
| Total | 140 |

The team would like to test the hypothesis at the 5% significance level that the medication errors occur with equal probabilities. What is the value of the test statistic for this hypothesis test?

a.  7.815

b.  1.96

c.  0

d.  4.514

53. What distribution does the test statistic used in the goodness-of-fit test follow?

a.  $t$

b.  chi-square

c.  $F$

d.  Normal

54. A study was done to compare the elasticity of a polymer mortar during a compression test at three different strain rates. Below is the ANOVA table for the statistical analysis. What is your conclusion at the 5% significance level?

| Source | dF | SS | MS | F |
|---|---|---|---|---|
| Strain rate | 2 | 0.1614 | 0.0807 | 1.70 |
| Error | 12 | 0.5688 | 0.0474 | |
| Total | 14 | 0.7302 | | |

a. Reject $H_0$, conclude that the three means are the same.

b. Reject $H_0$, conclude that at least one mean is different than the others.

c. Do not reject $H_0$, conclude that the three means are the same.

d. Do not reject $H_0$, conclude that at least one mean is different than the others.

55. Which of the following is not an assumption required for use and interpretation of a one-way ANOVA?

a. Homogeneity of variance

b. Observations are paired

c. Observations are independent

d. Observations are normally distributed

56. A two-way ANOVA hypothesis test was used to test the effects of two factors on a response variable. What conclusions can be made from the interaction plot below?

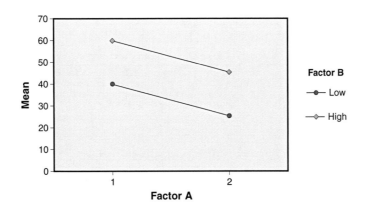

a. High levels of factor B tend to have smaller response values.

b. There is not an interaction effect between factors A and B.

c. There is an interaction effect between factors A and B.

d. Factors A and B do not have an effect on the response variable.

57. Consider the contingency table presented below. A hypothesis test for independence is conducted to determine if the number of nonconforming parts produced is independent of time of day. What type of distribution does the test statistic for this hypothesis test have?

| Time | Conforming parts | Nonconforming parts | Totals |
|---|---|---|---|
| Day | 94 | 5 | 99 |
| Evening | 87 | 10 | 97 |
| Overnight | 65 | 23 | 88 |
| Totals | 246 | 38 | 284 |

   a. $\chi^2$

   b. Normal

   c. Binomial

   d. Poisson

58. In the previous problem (question 57), the value of the test statistic for the hypothesis test is 19.071. What is the conclusion from this hypothesis test (use $\alpha = 0.05$)?

   a. Reject $H_0$, conclude that type of parts produced and time of day are independent.

   b. Reject $H_0$, conclude that type of parts produced and time of day are not independent.

   c. Do not reject $H_0$, conclude that type of parts produced and time of day are independent.

   d. Do not reject $H_0$, conclude that type of parts produced and time of day are not independent.

59. The fitted regression equation for two variables $x$ and $y$ is $\hat{y} = 2.5x - 8$. What is the slope of this equation?

   a. –8

   b. 1

   c. 2.5

   d. 0.89

60. A team wants to predict a person's cholesterol based on their weight in pounds. The fitted regression equation is Cholesterol = 140 + 0.23 × Weight. What is the predicted cholesterol of a person who weighs 130 pounds?

    a.  169.9

    b.  140

    c.  0.23

    d.  162.2

61. Paired data collected from a process are: (5.2, 26.7), (6.1, 27.5), (3.2, 24.9), (4.6, 25.5). What is the slope of the linear regression equation for these data?

    a.  0.92

    b.  0.96

    c.  21.74

    d.  −0.92

62. A study was done to predict people's cholesterol by their weight. A sample of 21 people was collected, and the linear regression equation was found to be Cholesterol = 140 + 0.20 × Weight. The team would like to determine if there is a significant linear relationship between weight and cholesterol. What is the appropriate alternative hypothesis for this statistical test?

    a.  $H_a : \beta_1 = 0$

    b.  $H_a : \beta_0 = 0$

    c.  $H_a : \beta_1 \neq 0$

    d.  $H_a : \beta_0 \neq 0$

63. The scatter plot below displays the relationship between two random variables. What is the correlation coefficient of these two variables?

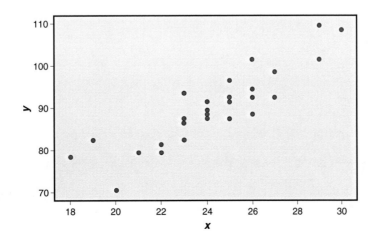

a.  0.88

b.  −0.88

c.  0

d.  1.40

64. The scatter plot below displays the relationship between two random variables. What is the correlation coefficient of these two variables?

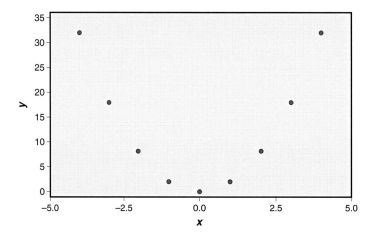

a.  −0.98

b.  0.98

c.  −0.98 and 0.98

d.  0

65. The fitted regression equation for two variables $x$ and $y$ is $\hat{y} = -5x + 131$. The coefficient of determination is 0.85, or 85%. What is the correlation coefficient?

a.  −0.92

b.  0.92

c.  0.85

d.  −1.45

66. The correlation coefficient between the age of a car and its cost is $r = -0.85$. This means that:

a.  changes in the age of the car cause the cost to change.

b.  as the age of a car increases, the cost of the car tends to increase.

c. as the age of a car increases, the cost of the car tends to decrease.

d. the cost of a car is controlled by its age.

67. When the measurement for one sample tends to be dependent on the measure for the previous sample, these data are called:

a. independent.

b. autocorrelated.

c. biased.

d. inconsistent.

68. Which of the following can help identify special cause variation in a process?

a. Statistical process control

b. Regression

c. Histogram

d. Capability analysis

69. A control chart was in control, but the operator adjusted the process anyway. What is this called?

a. Common cause variation

b. Special cause variation

c. Overcontrol

d. Undercontrol

70. What is the principal purpose of control charts?

a. To identify the source of special cause variation in a process

b. To adjust a process when it goes out of control

c. To automate a process

d. To help process operators recognize the presence of special causes of variation

71. Which of the following events would *not* be considered a source of common cause variation?

a. Measurement system variability

b. Incorrect machine settings

   c.  Variations in temperature

   d.  Slight changes in customer arrivals to a store

72.  Which of the following statements about rational subgrouping is correct?

   a.  Variability within samples is minimized.

   b.  Variability between samples is minimized.

   c.  Variability within samples is maximized.

   d.  There is no difference between within-sample variability and between-sample variability.

73.  Which quality leader introduced the use of control charts to monitor a quality characteristic?

   a.  Shewhart

   b.  Deming

   c.  Juran

   d.  Taguchi

74.  What probability distribution is required to construct $\bar{X}$ and $R$ control charts?

   a.  Binomial

   b.  Poisson

   c.  Normal

   d.  Uniform

75.  An $\bar{X}$ and $R$ chart was prepared for an operation using 25 samples with seven pieces in each sample. $\bar{\bar{X}}$ was found to be 24.8 and $\bar{R}$ was 5.50. During production, a sample of seven was taken and the pieces measured 25, 32, 35, 28, 27, 24, and 26. At the time this sample was taken:

   a.  both the average and range were within the control limits.

   b.  neither the average nor range were within the control limits.

   c.  only the average was outside the control limits.

   d.  only the range was outside the control limits.

76. The diameter of a steel rod is a quality characteristic of interest. Samples of size twelve will be selected in the subgroups. Which of the following control charts is preferred to monitor the process variability?

    a. $\bar{X}$ and $R$ chart

    b. $\bar{X}$ and $s$ chart

    c. $p$-chart

    d. $c$-chart

77. An $\bar{X}$ and $s$ chart was prepared for an operation using 25 samples with six pieces in each sample. $\bar{\bar{X}}$ was found to be 12.68 and $\bar{s}$ was 2.45. During production, a sample of six was taken and the pieces measured 11, 13, 14, 14, 10, and 12. At the time this sample was taken:

    a. both the average and standard deviation were within the control limits.

    b. neither the average nor standard deviation were within the control limits.

    c. only the average was outside the control limits.

    d. only the standard deviation was outside the control limits.

78. A company would like to monitor a continuous quality characteristic of a product. However, it is expensive to obtain the measurements of this quality characteristic. Which of the following control charts is most appropriate to monitor this process?

    a. I-MR chart

    b. $\bar{X}$ and $R$ chart

    c. $\bar{X}$ and $s$ chart

    d. $p$-chart

79. A hospital is monitoring the surgeries that result in surgical complications. The number of surgeries each month and those resulting in a complication were recorded. The number of surgeries each month can vary. Which of the following control charts is most appropriate to monitor this process?

    a. $\bar{X}$ and $R$ chart

    b. $p$-chart

    c. $np$-chart

    d. $c$-chart

80. A factory collected data on the number of nonconforming parts and constructed a $p$-chart. 15 samples of size 150 were collected. They determined that the average fraction of nonconforming parts was $\bar{p} = 0.037$. During production, a sample of 150 parts was taken, of which 11 were nonconforming. At the time this sample was taken:

   a. the sample was within the control limits.

   b. the sample was outside the control limits.

   c. the upper control limit was 0.073.

   d. the lower control limits was –0.01.

81. What is the upper control limit for a $p$-chart when the average daily production is 3575 units with an established fraction defective of 0.048?

   a. 0.0600

   b. 0.7053

   c. 0.0587

   d. 0.6893

82. A team at a factory would like to monitor the number of defects in a TV screen. Twenty-five samples of five TV screens are inspected. Which of the following control charts is most appropriate for this scenario?

   a. $\bar{X}$ and $R$ chart

   b. $p$-chart

   c. $np$-chart

   d. $c$-chart

83. A team at a factory is monitoring the average number of defects in TV screens. Thirty-five TV screens are randomly selected each day over a 25-day period. The average number of defects per TV screen was found to be $\bar{u} = 0.73$. What is the upper control limit for a corresponding $u$-chart?

   a. 1.24

   b. 0.30

   c. 1.16

   d. 0.22

84. A team would like to be able to detect small shifts in a process using a control chart. Which of the following control charts is most appropriate for this goal?

a. $\bar{X}$ and $R$ chart

b. $\bar{X}$ and $s$ chart

c. Individuals chart

d. CUSUM chart

85. If a process is out of control, the probability that a single point on the $\bar{X}$ chart will fall between plus two sigma and the upper control limit is:

a. 0.2240

b. 0.1587

c. 0.3413

d. Unknown

86. If a process is in control, it is desirable to:

a. adjust the process when a point is not on target.

b. have a small average run length.

c. have a large average run length.

d. stop monitoring the process.

87. Consider the following MR chart of a normally distributed process. What conclusions can be drawn from this control chart?

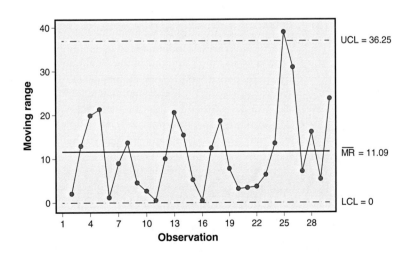

a. The process is out of control.

b. The process is stable.

c. The process is operating within the specifications.

d. The process is operating outside the specifications.

88. Consider the following *p*-chart. What conclusions can be drawn from this control chart?

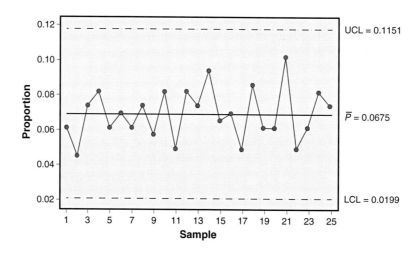

a. The process is out of control.

b. The process is stable.

c. The process is operating within the specifications.

d. The process is operating outside the specifications.

89. Consider the following $\overline{X}$ chart of a normally distributed process. What conclusions can be drawn from this control chart?

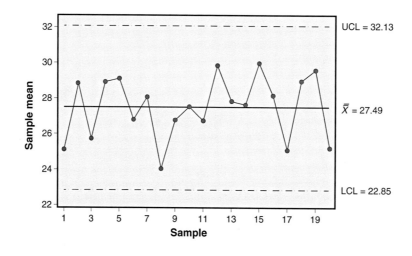

a. The process is out of control.

b. The process is stable.

c. The process is operating within the specifications.

d. The process is operating outside the specifications.

90. The main disadvantage of pre-control charts compared to a control chart is that:

a. the process is compared to a historic distribution in a pre-control chart.

b. pre-control charts are not statistically based.

c. pre-control charts are harder to construct than control charts.

d. pre-control charts are harder to interpret.

91. Which of the following is an advantage of pre-control charts?

a. Pre-control charts provide information on how a process can be brought back into control.

b. Pre-control charts provide information about how variability in a process can be reduced.

c. Pre-control charts can be used for processes whose capability ratio is less than one.

d. Pre-control charts are useful in setup operations to assess whether a product is produced between the tolerances.

92. A manufacturing company received an order for a build-to-order product from a customer. The company would like to monitor the process; which of the following tools is most appropriate?

a. Pre-control chart

b. $\bar{X}$ and $R$ control chart

c. Short-run SPC

d. Capability analysis

93. What is the first step in a capability study?

a. Compare the actual capability to the desired capability.

b. Measure the process capability.

c. Estimate the process parameters.

d. Verify that the process is stable.

94. A team would like to determine whether a process is able to meet customer specifications. What quality tool should they use?

    a. Flowchart

    b. Cause-and-effect diagram

    c. Capability analysis

    d. Regression analysis

95. The dimension of a component has specifications $5.5 \pm 0.25$. The process data are normally distributed with mean 5.45 and standard deviation 0.085. What fraction of components will have this dimension outside the specification limits?

    a. 0.9904

    b. 0.0096

    c. 0.9998

    d. 0.0002

96. The diameter of a stainless steel rod is an important quality characteristic. The rod has specifications $2.50 \pm 0.05$. Data from the process indicate the distribution is normally distributed, and an $\bar{X}$ and $R$ chart indicates the process is stable. The control charts used a sample of size 7 and found that $\bar{X} = 2.5014$ and $\bar{R} = 0.0568$. What fraction of steel rods are within the specification limits?

    a. 0.9825

    b. 0.0175

    c. 0.0071

    d. 0.9896

97. Which of the following is the correct formula to find the specification limits of a quality characteristic?

    a. $\mu \pm 3\sigma$

    b. $\bar{x} \pm 3\dfrac{\sigma}{\sqrt{n}}$

    c. $\dfrac{USL - LSL}{6\sigma}$

    d. Specification limits are determined externally and do not have a generic formula.

98. A stable, normally distributed process has specifications $21.35 \pm 4.50$. A sample of data from the process had a mean $\bar{X} = 20.98$ and standard deviation $\sigma = 1.10$. Find $C_p$ and $C_{pk}$.

   a. $C_p = 1.36$, $C_{pk} = 1.25$

   b. $C_p = 1.25$, $C_{pk} = 1.36$

   c. $C_p = 1.36$, $C_{pk} = 1.48$

   d. $C_p = 2.73$, $C_{pk} = 1.36$

99. A stable process has specifications $14 \pm 5$. The process is normally distributed with mean 13 and standard deviation 1.5. Is this process considered capable?

   a. Yes, since $C_p = 1.11$

   b. Yes, since $C_{pk} = 0.89$

   c. No, since $C_{pk} = 0.89$

   d. No, since $C_{pk} = 1.33$

100. The diameter of a stainless steel rod is an important quality characteristic. The rod has specifications $2.50 \pm 0.05$. Data from the process indicate the distribution is normally distributed, and an $\bar{X}$ and $R$ chart indicates the process is stable. The control charts used a sample of size 7 and found that $\bar{\bar{X}} = 2.5014$ and $\bar{R} = 0.0568$. What is the capability of this process?

   a. 0.79

   b. 0.77

   c. 0.82

   d. 0.98

101. Which of the following metrics is recommended to evaluate process capability when the process is not in statistical control?

   a. $C_p$

   b. $P_p$

   c. $C_{pk}$

   d. $C_r$

*Use the following scenario to answer the following three problems (questions 102–104).*

A textile company is designing an experiment to test the effects of temperature, pressure, and time on tensile properties of a fiber composite. Each of these factors will be run at a high and low level. A full-factorial design is used with four replicates per run.

102. How many treatment combinations are in this experiment?

    a.  3

    b.  9

    c.  8

    d.  4

103. How many factors are in this experiment?

    a.  3

    b.  4

    c.  2

    d.  12

104. Variation observed in the readings of the replicates for each treatment combination is referred to as what?

    a.  Interaction

    b.  Experimental error

    c.  Capability

    d.  Noise variable

105. What is the first step in designing a successful experiment?

    a.  Choose the factors and responses

    b.  Select the experimental design

    c.  Define the method of measurement

    d.  State the objective of the experiment

106. What technique in experimental design will reduce the effect of uncontrolled variables that are not part of the experiment but might affect the response variable?

    a.  Confounding

b. Blocking

c. Randomization

d. Interaction

107. An experiment is being conducted in a factory. Each experimental run takes several hours, so the experiment will last several days. What design technique would help in this experiment?

a. Confounding

b. Blocking

c. Randomization

d. Replication

108. Which of the following statements on randomized block designs is *not* true?

a. The blocking factor is not modeled as an interaction with treatments.

b. Determining whether the levels of the blocking factor are significant is not of interest.

c. We do not need to include a blocking variable in the designed experiment.

d. Including the blocking factor reduces its effect on the response.

109. Consider the ANOVA table below for a one-factor experiment with a blocking variable. What conclusions can be drawn from this ANOVA table?

| Source of variation | df | SS | MS | F | p-value |
|---|---|---|---|---|---|
| Factor A | 4 | 198.0 | 49.5 | 12.05 | 0.004 |
| Block | 3 | 101.75 | 33.92 | | |
| Error | 12 | 79.25 | 6.60 | | |
| Total | 19 | 379.0 | | | |

a. The blocking variable has a significant effect on the response.

b. Factor A has a significant effect on the response.

c. There is a significant interaction between factor A and the blocking variable.

d. Both the blocking variable and factor A have a significant effect on the response.

110. True/False. Once an experiment has been carried out with blocking included, we can reanalyze the experiment as if it were not blocked.

    a. True

    b. False

111. An experiment is being conducted on the yield of a substance. Two factors are believed to have an effect on the yield. What type of design would be appropriate for this experiment?

    a. Randomized block design

    b. Interaction

    c. Factorial design

    d. Latin square

112. Consider the following results of a $2^3$ full-factorial design. Assuming normality and equal variance assumptions are valid, which terms have a significant effect on the response variable?

| Source | df | SS | MS | F | p-value |
|--------|----|------|--------|--------|---------|
| A | 1 | 35.03 | 35.03 | 264.38 | 0.000 |
| B | 1 | 30.54 | 30.54 | 230.49 | 0.000 |
| C | 1 | 0.10 | 0.10 | 0.75 | 0.400 |
| AB | 1 | 2.98 | 2.98 | 22.49 | 0.001 |
| AC | 1 | 0.02 | 0.02 | 0.15 | 0.693 |
| BC | 1 | 0.03 | 0.03 | 0.23 | 0.646 |
| ABC | 1 | 0.002 | 0.002 | 0.15 | 0.902 |
| Error | 8 | 1.06 | 0.1325 | | |
| Total | 15 | 69.76 | | | |

    a. A and B only

    b. A, B, and AB

    c. All main effects

    d. C, AC, BC, and ABC

113. Which of the following graphical tools can help assess the assumption of independence when analyzing the results of a full-factorial design?

    a. Contour plot

    b. Normal probability plot

    c. Histogram

    d. Run chart

114. A $2^4$ full-factorial experiment is conducted with a single replicate. If all main effects and interactions are included in the model, how many degrees of freedom does the error term have?

    a. 15

    b. 1

    c. 8

    d. None

115. An experiment has eight factors at two levels each. The experiment has 128 runs. What is the experimental design called?

    a. Full-factorial design

    b. Half-fractional factorial design

    c. Taguchi design

    d. None of the above

116. An advantage of using a full-factorial design over a fractional factorial design is that:

    a. all main effects and two-factor interactions are estimable.

    b. it has projection properties.

    c. it requires fewer runs.

    d. effects are confounded.

117. In a resolution IV fractional factorial experiment, main effects are confounded with:

    a. three-factor and higher interactions.

    b. other main effects.

   c.  two-factor and higher interactions.

   d.  no other effects.

118.  Consider an experiment with five factors each at two levels. Using the defining relation I = ABD = ACE = BCDE, with which effects is main effect B aliased?

   a.  BD and CE

   b.  BC, DE, ABE, and ACD

   c.  AD and CDE

   d.  B is not aliased with other effects.

119.  An experiment is being conducted to find the optimal ingredients for a cake mix. The experimenters want the taste of the cake to be unaffected by small variations in oven temperature in the customers' homes. This is a problem of:

   a.  interaction.

   b.  confounding.

   c.  measurement error.

   d.  robustness.

120.  A team conducted an experiment to determine the optimal amount of three ingredients in a cake in order to maximize the taste. Two noise factors (oven temperature and baking time) were also included. A crossed-array design was used. The analysis indicated that there was a significant interaction between one of the ingredients and the oven temperature. Which of the following statements is true?

   a.  There is no robust design problem for this experiment.

   b.  It may be possible to find settings of the ingredients that are robust to the oven temperature.

   c.  The oven temperature does not have an effect on the taste of the cake.

   d.  The three ingredients are uncontrollable factors in this experiment.

## SOLUTIONS

  1.  a; Discrete data can only take on countable values. The result of the medical test is pass/fail. Errors in the medical record and the number of patient falls have possible values of 0, 1, 2, . . . . Patient weight can be an infinite number of values and is therefore continuous data. [VI.A.1]

2. c; Length, volume, and time can take on values over an interval of numbers. There are infinitely many values between any two values on their respective scales. Number of nonconforming components, however, can only take on a set of countable values, so it is discrete data. [VI.A.1]

3. a; The color of a car is classified into categories and there is no order implied. [VI.A.2]

4. d; Height has meaningful differences and an absolute zero exists. [VI.A.2]

5. b; Rating of a service is classified into categories where order is important. The precise difference between values is not defined. [VI.A.2]

6. b; When a population can be divided naturally into groups, it is often desirable to use stratified sampling. This will ensure that your sample is representative of the population. Double sampling and multiple sampling are sampling plans used for acceptance sampling. [VI.A.4]

7. c;

$$\bar{x} = \frac{5+8+12+3+2+7+6+5}{8} = 6 \text{ minutes}$$

The median is the value that divides the ordered data into two equal parts. The ordered data are: 2, 3, 5, 5, 6, 7, 8, 12. Since there is an even number of observations, the median is the average of the two central values. The location of the median is

$$\frac{n+1}{2} = \frac{9}{2} = 4.5. \ M = \frac{5+6}{2} = 5.5 \text{ minutes.}$$

[VI.A.5]

8. a;

$$\bar{x} = \frac{\sum_{i=1}^{n} x_i}{n} = \frac{3.2+3.1+3.4+3.1+3.2+3.3+3.2}{7} = 3.21486 \text{ in}$$

$$s = \sqrt{\frac{\sum_{i=1}^{n}(x_i - \bar{x})^2}{n-1}} = \sqrt{\frac{(3.2-3.21486)^2 + \ldots + (3.2-3.21486)^2}{7-1}} = \sqrt{\frac{0.06857}{6}} = 0.1069 \text{ in}$$

[VI.A.5]

9. c; The population mean and median are not equal, so the distribution can not be symmetric. The mean is sensitive to the data, while the median is a robust statistic and is not heavily influenced by extreme observations. Therefore, a much smaller mean indicates that the data are skewed to the left. [VI.A.5]

Part VI
Solutions

10. b; Under the central limit theorem, the distribution of sample averages tends toward a normal distribution as the sample size increases. Although the exponential distribution is right skewed, the distribution of sample averages is approximately normally distributed for large sample sizes. In this case $n = 40$. [VI.A.5]

11. c; The formula for the population variance is defined as

$$\sigma^2 = \frac{\sum_{i=1}^{N}(x_i - \mu)^2}{N}$$

Note that the sample variance is defined as

$$s^2 = \frac{\sum_{i=1}^{n}(x_i - \bar{x})^2}{n-1}$$

[VI.A.5]

12. b; Side-by-side box plots can be used to easily compare any differences between the wait times by day of the week. Histograms are more suited for describing the distribution of one population. Scatter plots are used to examine the relationship between two continuous variables. Probability plots are used to determine whether data follow a certain distribution, for example, the normal distribution. [VI.A.6]

13. c; A box plot divides a sorted data set into four regions. The lines in a box plot are marked by the minimum, Q1, median, Q3, and the maximum. The mean is not typically identified on a box plot. [VI.A.6]

14. a; A stem-and-leaf plot contains the values of every observation in the data set. A histogram, on the other hand, displays observations in groups/bins as frequencies or relative frequencies. Therefore, a stem-and-leaf plot provides more information than a histogram. For example, it is easy to determine the median of the data from a stem-and-leaf plot. However, it would not be possible to find the median with just a histogram. [VI.A.6]

15. a; A normal probability plot can help determine whether a set of data comes from a population with a normal distribution. The normal distribution is a reasonable model if the data points fall along a straight line. The data points in this normal probability plot do not fall in a straight line, so the normal distribution would *not* be an appropriate model for the time to failure. [VI.A.7]

16. d; The average temperature of 15 randomly selected cups of coffee is a *statistic*. A statistic is a characteristic of a sample and is used to estimate the population parameter. In this case, the sample mean temperature of the 15 cups of coffee can be used to estimate the temperature of all coffee served in the restaurant. [VI.B.1]

17. c; A *parameter* is a characteristic of a population. It is a quantity that describes characteristics of a population. The value of a population parameter is frequently unknown and must be estimated by a sample statistic. [VI.B.1]

18. d; Let $N$ be the event that a nonconforming part is made and let $O$ be the event that the part was made overnight. The given condition is that the part is made overnight, so we want

$$P(N|O) = \frac{P(N \cap O)}{P(O)} = \frac{23/284}{88/284} = 0.26$$

[VI.B.3]

19. b; P(Not defective) = 1 – P(Defective) = 1 – 0.02 = 0.98 [VI.B.3]

20. d; There is not enough information provided to determine the probability that both events A and B occur. If we knew that A and B were independent, then we could use the multiplication rule: $P(A \cap B) = P(A) \times P(B)$. [VI.B.3]

21. a; Since events A and B are mutually exclusive, they can not occur simultaneously. Therefore, $P(A \cap B) = 0$. Note that $P(A \cup B) = P(A) + P(B) = 0.40 + 0.13 = 0.53$ since A and B are mutually exclusive. Recall that probabilities only take on values between 0 and 1. [VI.B.3]

22. d; Let $T$ represent the time between arrivals. $T$ has an exponential distribution with mean $\mu = 5$ minutes. Since

$$\mu = \frac{1}{\lambda}, \ \lambda = \frac{1}{\mu} = \frac{1}{5} = .02$$

The cumulative density function for an exponentially distributed random variable $T$ is given by:

$$F(x) = P(T \le x) = 1 - e^{-\lambda x}$$

Therefore,

$$P(T < 3) = 1 - e^{-\lambda \times 3} = 1 - e^{-0.2 \times 3} = 1 - 0.5488 = 0.4512$$

[VI.C.1]

23. a; X has a normal distribution with mean μ = 15 and standard deviation σ = 2. The probability of interest is P(X > 18). Transform X into the random variable Z using the relationship

$$Z = \frac{X - \mu}{\sigma}$$

Then use a standard normal table to find the appropriate probability. From the properties of the cumulative distribution function, $P(X > a) = 1 - P(X < a)$.

$$P(X > 18) = P\left(\frac{X - \mu}{\sigma} > \frac{18 - 15}{2}\right) = P(Z > 1.50)$$

$$= 1 - P(Z < 1.50) = 1 - 0.9332 = 0.0668$$

[VI.C.1]

24. d; The normal distribution, *t*-distribution, and uniform distribution are all symmetric probability distributions. Asymmetric distributions include the exponential distribution, Weibull distribution, chi-square distribution, and lognormal distribution. [VI.C.1]

25. b; For overfilled, we would only want to examine the proportion of bottles with more than 24.08 oz. Let X represent the amount in a given bottle. Then we are looking for P(X > USL).

$$P(X > USL) = P(X > 24.08) = P\left(\frac{X - \mu}{\sigma} > \frac{24.08 - 24.01}{0.025}\right)$$

$$= P(Z > 2.80) = 1 - P(Z < 2.80) = 0.00256$$

[VI.C.1]

26. d; The *t*-distribution is symmetric, bell-shaped, and has mean μ = 0, like the standard normal distribution. However, the tails of the *t*-distribution are longer or heavier compared to the standard normal distribution. [VI.C.1]

27. c; Let X be the number of nonconforming units in a day. X has a Poisson distribution with rate λ = 5.

$$P(X \geq 2) = 1 - P(X \leq 1) = 1 - P(X = 0) - P(X = 1)$$

$$= 1 - \frac{e^{-5}5^0}{0!} - \frac{e^{-5}5^1}{1!}$$

$$= 1 - 0.0067 - 0.0337 = 0.9596$$

[VI.C.2]

28. a; The hypergeometric distribution is appropriate when the sample is taken without replacement from a finite population. The binomial distribution is appropriate when sampling is done with replacement. The normal distribution is not appropriate since it is a continuous probability distribution. [VI.C.2]

29 a; Let $X$ represent the number of invoices with an error. In this scenario, $X$ has a binomial distribution with $n = 15$ and $p = 0.10$. The probability of interest is $P(X = 4)$.

$$_nC_x = \binom{15}{4} = \frac{15!}{4!(15-4)!} = 1365$$

$$P(X = 4) = {}_nC_x p^x (1-p)^{n-x} = {}_{15}C_4 (0.10)^4 (1-0.10)^{15-4}$$

$$= 1365(0.0001)(0.3138) = 0.0428$$

[VI.C.2]

30. a;

$$E(X) = \mu_X = \Sigma x f(x) = 0(0.86) + 1(0.06) + 2(0.04) + 3(0.03) + 4(0.01) = 0.27$$

[VI.C.2]

31. c; The central limit theorem states that if the sample size $n$ is sufficiently large, then the sample mean $\bar{X}$ follows approximately a normal distribution with mean $\mu_{\bar{x}} = \mu$ and standard deviation $\sigma_{\bar{x}} = \sigma/\sqrt{n}$. In this case, $\mu = 24$, $\sigma = 5.5$, and $n = 32$. Therefore, $\mu_{\bar{x}} = \mu = 24$. [VI.C.2]

32. b; Since the underlying distribution is normal, then the sampling distribution of $\bar{X}$ also follows a normal distribution with mean $\mu_{\bar{x}} = \mu$ and standard deviation $\sigma_{\bar{x}} = \sigma/\sqrt{n}$. Note that the large sample size requirement is not necessary here since the filling process has a normal distribution. In this population, $\mu = 24$, $\sigma = 0.05$, and $n = 16$. Therefore, $\mu_{\bar{x}} = 24$ and $\sigma_{\bar{x}} = \sigma/\sqrt{n} = 0.05/\sqrt{16} = 0.0125$.

The probability of interest is

$$P(\bar{X} > 24.04) = P\left(\frac{\bar{X} - \mu_{\bar{x}}}{\sigma_{\bar{x}}} > \frac{24.04 - 24}{0.05/\sqrt{16}}\right) = P(Z > 3.20)$$

$$= 1 - P(Z < 3.20) = 1 - 0.9993 = 0.0007$$

[VI.C.2]

Part VI
Solutions

33. b; In this problem $\mu = 58$, $\sigma^2 = 64$, and $n = 16$. The standard error is defined as

$$\text{s.e.}(\overline{X}) = \sigma / \sqrt{n} = \sqrt{64} / \sqrt{16} = 8/4 = 2.$$

[VI.D.1]

34. d; When we construct a confidence interval on a population parameter (in this case the population proportion $p$), then either the interval contains the true value of $p$ (probability of 1) or not (probability of 0). Recall that we do not know the true value of the population proportion. Answer (b) describes the practical interpretation of the confidence interval: with 95% confidence, we believe that the population proportion will lie between 0.02 and 0.12. [VI.D.1]

35. a; 11.73 mm is a point estimate for the average length of the component. Recall that a parameter is a characteristic of a population. The sample mean is often a point estimator for the population mean. [VI.D.1]

36. d; The population variance is unknown, so we use the sample standard deviation to estimate the population standard deviation. The $100(1 - \alpha)\%$ confidence interval for $\mu$ then is

$$\overline{x} - t_{\alpha/2,n-1} \frac{s}{\sqrt{n}} \leq \mu \leq \overline{x} + t_{\alpha/2,n-1} \frac{s}{\sqrt{n}}$$

$$\overline{x} = 4.3, \ s = 0.51, \ n = 15, \ \alpha/2 = 0.005, \ t_{0.005,14} = 2.977$$

$$4.3 - 2.977 \left( \frac{0.51}{\sqrt{15}} \right) \leq \mu \leq 4.3 + 2.977 \left( \frac{0.51}{\sqrt{15}} \right)$$

$$3.908 \leq \mu \leq 4.692$$

We are 95% confident that the mean tensile strength is between 3.908 and 4.692 MPa. [VI.D.1]

37. a; As stated in the problem, the estimate should be within 0.15 MPa of the true average. This means we will allow the estimate to be at most 0.15 MPa less than the average, or at most 0.15 MPa greater than the true average. So, the margin of error is $E = 0.15$. Furthermore, $\sigma = 0.50$, $\alpha = 0.05$, $Z_{\alpha/2} = Z_{.025} = 1.96$. The minimum sample size needed is

$$n \geq \left( \frac{\sigma Z_{\alpha/2}}{E} \right)^2 = \left( \frac{0.50(1.96)}{0.15} \right)^2 = 42.68$$

Therefore, the minimum sample size of cement would be $n = 43$. [VI.D.1]

38. d;

$$\bar{x} = \frac{\sum_{i=1}^{n} x_i}{n} = \frac{10.37 + 11.50 + 9.80 + 10.65 + 11.95 + 10.15 + 9.52}{7} = 10.563 \text{ V}$$

$$s^2 = \frac{\sum_{i=1}^{n} (x_i - \bar{x})^2}{n-1} = \frac{(10.37 - 10.563)^2 + \ldots + (9.52 - 10.563)^2}{7 - 1} = \frac{4.687}{6} = 0.781 \text{ V}^2$$

The $100(1 - \alpha)\%$ two-sided confidence interval on the population variance $\sigma^2$ is given by

$$\frac{(n-1)s^2}{\chi^2_{\alpha/2,k}} < \sigma^2 < \frac{(n-1)s^2}{\chi^2_{1-\alpha/2,k}}$$

$$n = 7, \ s^2 = 0.781, \ \alpha = 0.05, \ k = n - 1 = 6, \ \chi^2_{0.025,6} = 14.449, \ \chi^2_{0.975,6} = 1.237$$

$$\frac{(7-1)0.781}{14.449} < \sigma^2 < \frac{(7-1)0.781}{1.237}$$

$$0.324 < \sigma^2 < 3.788$$

We are 95% confident the true population variance of the voltage of the power supply lies within 0.324 V² and 3.788 V². [VI.D.1]

39. c; A one-sample $t$-test is appropriate where $H_0 : \mu = 18$ and $H_a : \mu \neq 18$. The test statistic for this hypothesis test is

$$t_0 = \frac{\bar{x} - \mu_0}{s / \sqrt{n}} = \frac{17.98 - 18}{0.03 / \sqrt{24}} = -3.266$$

Note: We will reject $H_0$ if $t_0 < -t_{\alpha/2,n-1}$ or $t_0 > t_{\alpha/2,n-1} = t_{0.025,23} = 2.069$.

Since $-3.266 < -2.069$, we reject $H_0$ and conclude that the mean volume of soda is not equal to 18 oz. [VI.D.2]

40. b; The $p$-value for the hypothesis test is 0.003, which is less than the significance level 0.05. Therefore, we have sufficient evidence to reject the null hypothesis and conclude that the mean volume is different than 18 oz. A 95% confidence interval of the population mean, therefore, would *not* contain 18. [VI.D.2]

41. c; The appropriate hypothesis test is a $t$-test since it is a test for a single population mean $\mu$ and the population variance $\sigma^2$ is unknown. A left-tailed test is appropriate, since the team would like to assess whether the mean is 25 mph or less. Note: The hypotheses for this test are $H_0 : \mu = 25$ versus $H_a : \mu < 25$. The test statistic is

$$t_0 = \frac{\bar{x} - \mu}{s/\sqrt{n}} = \frac{24.50 - 25}{2.3/\sqrt{20}} = -0.97$$

Using a significance level of 5%, we will reject $H_0$ if $t_0 < t_{\alpha,n-1} = -t_{0.05,19} = -1.729$. Since $-0.97 > -1.729$, we can not reject $H_0$. There is not sufficient evidence to conclude that the mean speed is less than 25 mph. [VI.D.2]

42.  c; Let $p$ be the true proportion of patient falls in the hospital. $x$ = The number of patient falls = 7. $n$ = Sample size = 56. The sample proportion is then

$$\hat{p} = \frac{x}{n} = \frac{7}{56} = 0.125.$$

The null and alternative hypotheses are $H_0 : p = 0.10$ versus $H_a : p > 0.10$. The significance level is $\alpha = 0.05$. This is a right-tailed test, so we reject the null hypothesis if the test statistic is greater than $z_\alpha = z_{0.05} = 1.645$. The test statistic is

$$z_0 = \frac{\hat{p} - p_0}{\sqrt{\dfrac{p_0(1-p_0)}{n}}} = \frac{0.125 - 0.10}{\sqrt{\dfrac{0.10(1-0.10)}{56}}} = 0.624$$

Since $0.624 < 1.645$, there is not enough evidence to reject $H_0$. At the 5% significance level, there is not enough evidence to conclude that the proportion of patient falls is more than 0.10. [VI.D.2]

43.  a; The parameter of interest is the difference in average fill volume, $\mu_1 - \mu_2$. The null and alternative hypotheses for the corresponding hypothesis test are $H_0 : \mu_1 - \mu_2 = 0$ versus $H_a : \mu_1 - \mu_2 \neq 0$. Note that the hypothesized value $\Delta_0 = 0$ is not contained in the confidence interval. Therefore, there is evidence that there is a difference in the two population means. [VI.D.2]

44.  b; The null and alternative hypotheses for this hypothesis test are $H_0 : \mu_{\text{Before}} - \mu_{\text{After}} = 0$ versus $H_a : \mu_{\text{Before}} - \mu_{\text{After}} > 0$. The significance level is $\alpha = 0.01$. This is a right-tailed test, so we will reject the null hypothesis if the test statistic is greater than $t_{\alpha,k} = t_{0.01,n_1+n_2-2} = t_{0.01,50} = 2.403$. Note that the test statistic is

$$t_0 = \frac{\bar{x}_{\text{Before}} - \bar{x}_{\text{After}} - 0}{\sqrt{\dfrac{s^2_{\text{Before}}}{n_{\text{Before}}} + \dfrac{s^2_{\text{After}}}{n_{\text{After}}}}} = \frac{3.52 - 2.10 - 0}{\sqrt{\dfrac{2.34}{28} + \dfrac{2.04}{25}}} = 3.494$$

Since $3.494 > 2.403$, we reject $H_0$ and conclude that there is a significant difference in the packaging time. [VI.D.2]

45. d; Let $\sigma_1^2$ represent the population variance of the packaging time before the improvement project, and let $\sigma_2^2$ represent the population variance of the packaging time after the improvement project. The null and alternative hypotheses are

$$H_0: \sigma_1^2 = \sigma_2^2 \text{ versus } H_a: \sigma_1^2 \neq \sigma_2^2.$$

The test statistic is

$$F_0 = \frac{s_1^2}{s_2^2} = \frac{2.34}{2.04} = 1.147.$$

Note that this is a two-tailed test with significance level $\alpha = 0.10$. The degrees of freedom are $k_1 = n_1 - 1 = 27$ and $k_2 = n_2 - 1 = 24$. The critical values are:

$$F_{\alpha/2,k_1,k_2} = F_{0.05,27,24} = 1.93$$

and

$$F_{1-\alpha/2,k_1,k_2} = F_{0.95,27,24} = \frac{1}{F_{\alpha/2,k_2,k_1}} = \frac{1}{F_{0.05,24,27}} = \frac{1}{1.96} = 0.51.$$

We will reject $H_0$ if

$$F_0 < F_{1-\alpha/2,k_1,k_2} \text{ or } F_0 > F_{\alpha/2,k_1,k_2}.$$

Since $1.147 > 0.51$ and $1.147 < 1.93$, we do not reject $H_0$ and conclude there is no significant change in the variance of packaging time before and after the performance improvement project. [VI.D.2]

46. a; Let $p_1$ represent the proportion of nonconforming units produced by machine 1 and $p_2$ represent the proportion of nonconforming units produced by machine 2.

$$x_1 = 28, \; n_1 = 1250, \; \hat{p}_1 = \frac{x_1}{n_1} = \frac{28}{1250} = 0.0224$$

$$x_2 = 18, \; n_2 = 1175, \; \hat{p}_2 = \frac{x_2}{n_2} = \frac{18}{1175} = 0.015319$$

$\hat{p}$ is the estimate of the overall proportion for the parameter $p_1 - p_2$.

$$\hat{p} = \frac{x_1 + x_2}{n_1 + n_2} = \frac{28+18}{1250+1175} = \frac{46}{2425} = 0.01897$$

The level of significance is $\alpha = 0.10$. $z_{\alpha/2} = z_{0.05} = 1.645$.

A $100(1 - \alpha)\%$ confidence interval on the parameter $p_1 - p_2$ is

$$(\hat{p}_1 - \hat{p}_2) - z_{\alpha/2}\sqrt{\hat{p}(1-\hat{p})\left(\frac{1}{n_1} + \frac{1}{n_2}\right)} \le p_1 - p_2 \le (\hat{p}_1 - \hat{p}_2) + z_{\alpha/2}\sqrt{\hat{p}(1-\hat{p})\left(\frac{1}{n_1} + \frac{1}{n_2}\right)}$$

$$(0.0224 - 0.015319) - 1.645\sqrt{0.01897(1-0.01897)\left(\frac{1}{1250} + \frac{1}{1175}\right)} \le p_1 - p_2 \le$$

$$(0.0224 - 0.015319) + 1.645\sqrt{0.01897(1-0.01897)\left(\frac{1}{1250} + \frac{1}{1175}\right)}$$

$$-0.002 \le p_1 - p_2 \le 0.016.$$

We are 90% confident that the difference between the proportion of nonconforming parts is between −0.002 and 0.016. Because 0 is contained in this confidence interval, there is not sufficient evidence to conclude that the two machines have a different proportion of nonconforming parts. [VI.D.2]

47. d; $\beta$ = P(Type II error) = 1 − Power = 1 − 0.80 = 0.20. The significance level is $\alpha$ = P(Type I error). [VI.D.2]

48. c; A type II error occurs when $H_0$ is not rejected when in fact $H_0$ is false. A type I error occurs when $H_0$ is rejected when in fact $H_0$ is true. [VI.D.2]

49. a; We would use a two-sample $p$-test to compare the proportions of defective widgets from two machines. The test statistic for this test is

$$z_0 = \frac{\hat{p}_1 - \hat{p}_2}{\sqrt{\hat{p}(1-\hat{p})\left(\frac{1}{n_1} + \frac{1}{n_2}\right)}},$$

where

$$\hat{p} = \frac{x_1 + x_2}{n_1 + n_2}.$$

This test statistic follows a standard normal distribution for sufficiently large sample sizes. [VI.D.2]

50. a; A paired $t$-test is most appropriate because the same individuals were measured twice. There is a strong relationship between the two measurements. [VI.D.3]

51. b; A paired *t*-test is required for this hypothesis test because there is a relationship between two observations. The same component was measured twice, once by each inspector. Therefore, we can perform a hypothesis test on the difference between the length measured by inspector A and the length measured by inspector B.

| Component | 1 | 2 | 3 | 4 | 5 |
|---|---|---|---|---|---|
| Inspector A | 10.2 | 9.8 | 10.1 | 10.3 | 10.4 |
| Inspector B | 10.0 | 9.9 | 10.3 | 10.0 | 10.3 |
| $d_i = A_i - B_i$ | 0.2 | –0.1 | –0.2 | 0.3 | 0.1 |

Let $\mu_1$ represent the mean length measured by inspector A and let $\mu_2$ represent the mean length measured by inspector B. Let $\mu_D$ represent the true mean difference between the two populations. $\mu_D = \mu_1 - \mu_2$.

The necessary summary statistics are

$$\bar{d} = \frac{\Sigma_{i=1}^n d_i}{n} = \frac{0.2 + (-0.1) + (-0.2) + (0.3) + (0.1)}{5} = 0.06$$

$$s_d = \sqrt{\frac{\Sigma_{i=1}^n (d_i - \bar{d})^2}{n-1}} = \sqrt{\frac{(0.2 - 0.06)^2 + \ldots + (0.1 - 0.06)^2}{5-1}} = 0.2074.$$

The null and alternative hypotheses are $H_0 : \mu_D = 0$ versus $H_a : \mu_D \neq 0$. The significance level is $\alpha = 0.01$. This is a two-tailed test, so we will reject $H_0$ if the test statistic is less than $-t_{\alpha/2,k}$ or greater than $t_{\alpha/2,k} = -t_{0.005,n-1} = t_{0.005,4} = 4.604$. The test statistic is

$$t_0 = \frac{\bar{d}}{s_d / \sqrt{n}} = \frac{0.06}{0.2074 / \sqrt{5}} = 0.65.$$

Since $0.65 < 4.604$, we do not reject $H_0$ and conclude there is not a significant difference between the mean length measured by the two inspectors. [VI.D.3]

52. d; A goodness-of-fit test is appropriate here. The team would like to test whether the medication errors occur with equal probabilities. Therefore, the null and alternative hypotheses are $H_0 : p_1 = p_2 = p_3 = p_4 = 0.25$ versus $H_a : p_i \neq 0.25$ for at least one $i = 1, 2, 3, 4$.

The test statistic is

$$\chi_0^2 = \Sigma_{i=1}^k \frac{(O_i - E_i)^2}{E_i},$$

where $E_i = (140)(0.25) = 35$ for $i = 1, 2, 3, 4$. Therefore,

$$\chi_0^2 = \frac{(32-35)^2}{35} + \frac{(28-35)^2}{35} + \frac{(45-35)^2}{35} + \frac{(35-35)^2}{35} = 4.514.$$

Note that for a significance level $\alpha = 0.05$, we will reject $H_0$ if

$$\chi_0^2 > \chi_{\alpha,k-1}^2 = \chi_{0.05,3}^2 = 7.81.$$

Since $4.514 < 7.81$, we do not reject $H_0$ and conclude that the medication errors occur with equal probabilities. [VI.D.4]

53. b; The test statistic for a goodness-of-fit test is defined as

$$\chi_0^2 = \Sigma_{i=1}^k \frac{(O_i - E_i)^2}{E_i}.$$

The test statistic follows a chi-square distribution with $k - 1$ degrees of freedom where $k$ is the number of categories. [VI.D.4]

54. c; From the ANOVA table and using an $F$ table, we can find the critical value and compare it to the test statistic $F_0 = 1.70$. From the ANOVA table, the degrees of freedom for the critical value are 2 and 12. From an $F$ table, we can find $F_{0.05,2,12} = 19.41$. Since $F_0 < 19.41$, we do not reject $H_0$ and conclude that there is not a significant difference between the three means. [VI.D.5]

55. b; The assumptions for a one-way ANOVA are that the observations follow a normal distribution, the observations are independent, and the treatments have constant variance. Paired data is not an assumption for ANOVA. [VI.D.5]

56. b; An interaction plot can show you differences in the mean response for the different levels of factors A and B. This interaction plot indicates that there is no significant interaction between factors A and B. As you move across the levels of factor A, the levels of factor B maintain identical patterns. Note that high levels of factor B tend to have higher values of the response, not smaller levels of the response. [VI.D.5]

57. a; The test statistic for a test of independence is

$$\chi_0^2 = \Sigma_{i=1}^r \Sigma_{j=1}^c \frac{\left(O_{ij} - E_{ij}\right)^2}{E_{ij}}.$$

This test statistic follows a chi-square distribution with $(r-1)(c-1)$ degrees of freedom. [VI.D.6]

58. b; The test statistic for the test of independence follows a chi-square distribution with $(r-1)(c-1)$ degrees of freedom, where $r$ represents the number of levels of the first factor and $c$ represents the number of levels of the second factor. We reject $H_0$ if

$$\chi_0^2 > \chi_{\alpha,(r-1)(c-1)}^2 = \chi_{0.05,2} = 5.991.$$

Since

$$\chi_0^2 = 19.071 > 5.991,$$

we reject $H_0$ and conclude that the type of part produced (conforming or nonconforming) and time of day are not independent. [VI.D.6]

59. c; The slope represents the change in the response $y$ for every one unit change in the variable $x$. Therefore, 2.5 is the slope of the fitted regression equation. [VI.E.1]

60. a; By plugging in the given value of Weight = 130 into the regression equation, we can predict the cholesterol. Cholesterol = 140 + 0.23 × (130) = 169.9. [VI.E.1]

61. a;

|   | $x$ | $y$ | $xy$ | $x^2$ | $y^2$ |
|---|---|---|---|---|---|
|   | 5.2 | 26.7 | 138.84 | 27.04 | 712.89 |
|   | 6.1 | 27.5 | 167.75 | 37.21 | 756.25 |
|   | 3.2 | 24.9 | 79.68 | 10.24 | 620.01 |
|   | 4.6 | 25.5 | 117.3 | 21.16 | 650.25 |
| Σ | 19.1 | 104.6 | 503.57 | 95.65 | 2739.40 |
| Mean | 4.775 | 26.15 |   |   |   |

$$S_{xx} = \sum_{i=1}^{4} x_i^2 - \frac{\left(\Sigma_{i=1}^4 x_i\right)^2}{n} = 95.65 - \frac{(19.1)^2}{4} = 4.4475$$

$$S_{xy} = \sum_{i=1}^{4} x_i y_i - \frac{\left(\Sigma_{i=1}^4 x_i\right)\left(\Sigma_{i=1}^4 y_i\right)}{n} = 503.57 - \frac{(19.1)(104.6)}{4} = 4.105$$

The slope of the regression equation can be found using the formula

$$b_1 = \frac{S_{xy}}{S_{xx}} = \frac{4.105}{4.4475} = 0.923.$$

Note that

$$b_0 = \bar{y} - b_1\bar{x} = 26.15 - (0.923)(4.775) = 21.74.$$

Therefore, the full regression equation is

$$\hat{y} = 21.74 + 0.923x.$$

[VI.E.1]

62. c; The appropriate test is a hypothesis test on the slope of the linear regression equation, not the intercept of the linear regression equation. The slope is represented by $\beta_1$ and the intercept is represented by $\beta_0$. The null hypothesis is $H_0 : \beta_1 = 0$. The alternative hypothesis is $H_a : \beta_1 \neq 0$. [VI.E.1]

63. a; The sample correlation coefficient measures the strength of the linear relationship between two variables. The scatter plot shows that as $x$ increases, $y$ increases. This indicates that there is a positive correlation. The correlation coefficient only takes values between –1 and +1. The closer the value is to –1 or +1, the stronger the linear relationship, so there is a strong positive correlation between these two variables. [VI.E.2]

64. d; The sample correlation coefficient measures the strength of the *linear* relationship between two variables. The scatter plot indicates that there is a quadratic relationship between the two variables, but this relationship is not linear. Therefore, the correlation coefficient $r$ is 0. [VI.E.2]

65. a; The correlation coefficient

$$r = \pm\sqrt{R^2}.$$

The coefficient of determination is $R^2 = 0.85$. The slope of the regression equation is –5, indicating that there is a negative linear relationship between $x$ and $y$. Therefore the correlation coefficient is

$$r = -\sqrt{0.85} = -0.92.$$

[VI.E.2]

66. c; Since the correlation coefficient is negative, there is an inverse linear association between the age and cost of the car. As the age of the car increases, the cost tends to decrease. Note that although there is a linear correlation, this does not imply that there is a causal relationship. An increase in the age of the car does not cause the cost to decrease. [VI.E.2]

67. b; Data that are autocorrelated means that the data in the previous sample affect the data in the next sample. [VI.E.3]

68. a; Statistical process control is a statistical technique that can help identify special cause variation. Regression analysis describes the relationship between one or more predictor variables and a response variable. Histograms are used to visualize data. Capability analysis is used to determine if a process is able to meet certain requirements. [VI.F.1]

69. c; Overcontrol, also called *overadjustment*, occurs when a process operator tries to adjust a process in response to common cause variation. In this scenario, the control chart has not indicated out-of-control behavior, but the operator adjusted the process anyway. [VI.F.2]

70. d; Control charts indicate whether a process is out of control, but they can not identify what caused the out-of-control behavior. Control charts do not automatically adjust the process. It is necessary for the process operator to determine and correct out-of-control behavior when it is indicated by a control chart. [VI.F.2]

71. b; Common cause variability is variation that is inherent in the process and not controllable by operators. Variation in ambient temperature, the measurement system, and customer arrivals are natural variability in a process. An incorrect setting on a machine, however, is an unusual event that can be adjusted by the operator. An incorrect setting is not inherent to the process and thus is a source of special cause variation. [VI.F.2]

72. a; Rational subgrouping involves selecting samples such that if there is special cause variation present in the process, there will be a greater probability of variation between samples, while the variation within samples is small. Therefore, the variability within samples is minimized and the variability between samples is maximized. [VI.F.4]

73. a; Walter A. Shewhart introduced the concept of control charts in the 1920s. [VI.F.5]

Part VI
Solutions

74. c; $\bar{X}$, $R$, $s$, $I$, and MR control charts require that the data under observation follow a normal distribution. Violations of this assumption will lead to poor performance of the control charts, particularly with I-MR charts. [VI.F.5]

75. b; The summary statistics for the sample are

$$\bar{x} = \frac{25+32+35+28+27+24+26}{7} = 28.14; \ R = 35-24 = 11.$$

From the information given,

$$\bar{\bar{x}} = 24.8, \ \bar{R} = 5.50, \ n = 7.$$

The control limits for the $\bar{X}$ chart are:

$$UCL = \bar{\bar{x}} + A_2\bar{R} = 24.8 + 0.419(5.50) = 27.10$$

$$LCL = \bar{\bar{x}} - A_2\bar{R} = 24.8 - 0.419(5.50) = 22.50$$

The control limits for the $R$ chart are:

$$UCL = D_4\bar{R} = (1.924)(5.50) = 10.58$$

$$LCL = D_3\bar{R} = (0.076)(5.50) = 0.418$$

$A_2$, $D_3$, and $D_4$ can be found in Appendix C of *The Certified Quality Engineer Handbook*, Third Edition for $n = 7$.

Therefore, since $\bar{X} = 28.14$ is greater than the UCL for the $\bar{X}$ chart, and $R = 11$ is greater than the UCL for the $R$ chart, neither the average nor range were within the control limits. [VI.F.5]

76. b; The diameter of the steel rod is variables data. Therefore, the *p*-chart and *c*-chart are not appropriate to monitor process variability. The sample size is relatively large ($n = 12$); therefore, the sample standard deviation is a better estimate of the process standard deviation compared to the range. In general, the sample standard deviation should be used instead of the range in estimating process variability. [VI.F.5]

77. a; The summary statistics for the sample are

$$\bar{x} = \frac{11+13+14+14+10+12}{6} = 12.33; \ s = \sqrt{\frac{(11-12.33)^2 + ... + (12-12.33)^2}{6-1}} = 1.633.$$

From the information given,

$$\bar{\bar{x}} = 12.68,\ \bar{s} = 2.45,\ n = 6$$

The control limits for the $\bar{X}$ chart are:

$$\text{UCL} = \bar{\bar{x}} + A_3\bar{s} = 12.68 + 1.287(2.45) = 15.83$$

$$\text{LCL} = \bar{\bar{x}} - A_3\bar{s} = 12.68 - 1.287(2.45) = 9.53$$

The control limits for the s-chart are:

$$\text{UCL} = B_4\bar{s} = (1.970)(2.45) = 4.83$$

$$\text{LCL} = B_3\bar{s} = (0.03)(2.45) = 0.07$$

$A_3$, $B_3$, and $B_4$ can be found in Appendix C of *The Certified Quality Engineer Handbook*, Third Edition for $n = 6$.

Since $\bar{X} = 12.33$ is within the UCL and LCL for the $\bar{X}$ chart, and $s = 1.633$ is within the UCL and LCL for the s-chart, both the average and standard deviation were within the control limits. [VI.F.5]

78. a; Because it is expensive to obtain the measurement of the quality characteristic, the subgroup should consist of a single observation ($n = 1$). Therefore, I-MR control charts are appropriate. Note that the quality characteristic is continuous, thus the $p$-chart is not appropriate. [VI.F.5]

79. b; The quality characteristic of interest is whether or not a surgery had a complication. This is attribute data, so an $\bar{X}$ and $R$ chart is not appropriate. A $c$-chart is also not appropriate as that control chart monitors nonconformities. Because the number of surgeries can vary each month, the $p$-chart is preferred over the $np$-chart. While $np$-charts are often easier to interpret, they should be used when the sample sizes are the same to avoid misleading results. [VI.F.5]

80. a; From the information provided, $\bar{p} = 0.037$, $m = 15$, $n = 150$.

The new sample fraction nonconforming is

$$\hat{p} = \frac{x}{n} = \frac{11}{150} = 0.073.$$

The control limits for the $p$-chart are

$$\text{UCL} = \bar{p} + 3\sqrt{\frac{\bar{p}(1-\bar{p})}{n}} = 0.037 + 3\sqrt{\frac{(0.037)(1-0.037)}{150}} = 0.083$$

$$\text{LCL} = \bar{p} - 3\sqrt{\frac{\bar{p}(1-\bar{p})}{n}} = 0.037 - 3\sqrt{\frac{(0.037)(1-0.037)}{150}} = -0.01 \to 0.$$

Since $\hat{p} = 0.073$ lies within the UCL and LCL of the p-chart, the sample is within the control limits. Note that the formula for the LCL leads to a negative number. By convention, this value is changed to 0 since you can not have a negative proportion. [VI.F.5]

81. c; From the information provided, $\hat{p} = 0.048$, $n = 3575$.

$$\text{UCL} = \bar{p} + 3\sqrt{\frac{\bar{p}(1-\bar{p})}{n}} = 0.048 + 3\sqrt{\frac{(0.048)(1-0.048)}{3575}} = 0.0587$$

[VI.F.5]

82. d; Defects on TVs are nonconformities. This is attribute data, so the $\bar{X}$ and $R$ charts are not appropriate. A control chart for nonconformities, the c-chart, is appropriate here. Note that the p- and np-charts are for fraction nonconforming. [VI.F.5]

83. c; From the information provided,

$$\bar{u} = 0.73, \ n = 35, \ m = 25$$

$$\text{UCL} = \bar{u} + 3\sqrt{\frac{\bar{u}}{n}} = 0.73 + 3\sqrt{\frac{0.73}{35}} = 1.16.$$

[VI.F.5]

84. d; A CUSUM control chart is more sensitive to small shifts in the process because it is based on the current observation and the most recent past observations. Shewhart control charts are known to be poor at detecting small shifts in the process mean because they are only based on the current observation. [VI.F.5]

85. d; Since the process is unstable (out of statistical control), the actual probability that a point lies within this region is unknown. [VI.F.6]

86. c; The average run length is the number of cycles, time periods, or samples that elapse before the process signals out of control. When the process is in control, we want the average run length to be large. If the process is in control, operators should not adjust the process if a point is not right on target. This overadjustment can destabilize a stable process. [VI.F.6]

87. a; A point is above the upper control limit, indicating that the process is out of statistical control. Note that a control chart does not provide information on whether the process is operating within the specification limits. A process could be out of statistical control, but still operating within the specification limits. Similarly, a process could be in control, but not be within the specification limits. [VI.F.6]

88. a; Beginning with the fourth data point, there is a sequence of 16 points alternating up and down. One of the sensitizing rules to detect out-of-control behavior is that there are fourteen points in a row alternating up and down. Note that a control chart does not provide information on whether the process is operating within the specification limits. A process could be out of statistical control, but still operating within the specification limits. Similarly, a process could be in control, but not be within the specification limits. [VI.F.6]

89. b; There is no unusual behavior indicated in the control chart; therefore, the process is in control (stable). Note that a control chart does not provide information on whether the process is operating within the specification limits. A process could be out of statistical control, but still operating within the specification limits. Similarly, a process could be in control, but not be within the specification limits. [VI.F.6]

90. b; Pre-control charts are not statistically based. The upper and lower pre-control limits are calculated from the tolerance limits. The standard method to find the pre-control limits is to multiply the tolerance by 0.25 and add this value to both the upper specification limit and the lower specification limit. However, a signal that the process is out of control does not necessarily indicate a high probability that the process has changed, leading to more overadjustment compared to control charts. [VI.F.7]

91. d; Pre-control charts are most useful in initial setup operations. At this point in the operation, there may not be enough data collected to construct a control chart. Pre-control charts can help determine whether the product being produced is centered between the tolerances. Pre-control charts do not provide information on how variability can be reduced or how to bring a process into control. They should also only be used for processes with a capability ratio greater than one. Poor capability in a pre-control chart will indicate that assignable causes of variation are present when in fact there are no assignable causes. [VI.F.7]

92. c; The factory has received a built-to-order product. This is not a process that has a long, continuous production run. Therefore, the classical control charts (for example, $\bar{X}$ and $R$) are not appropriate for monitoring the process variability. Short-run statistical process control is necessary. Standardized control charts are typically used for short-run processes. [VI.F.8]

93. d; The first step in a capability study is to verify that the process is stable. A stable process is one that does not have any special causes of variation present. If the process is not stable, the capability measures will not be valid estimates of the process capability. [VI.G.1]

94. c; Capability analysis is used to determine whether a process is capable of meeting requirements. The capability of a process can also be evaluated through use of histograms, probability plots, and stem-and-leaf plots. [VI.G.1]

95. b; Let X represent the dimension of the component. The upper specification limit is 5.75 and the lower specification limit is 5.25. First, consider the proportion of components that are within the specification limits. This can be written as P(5.25 < X < 5.75). Since the dimension is normally distributed, we can use the standard normal distribution to determine this fraction:

$$P(LSL < X < USL) = P(X < 5.25 < 5.75) = P\left(\frac{5.25 - 5.45}{0.085} < \frac{X - \bar{x}}{\hat{\sigma}} < \frac{5.75 - 5.45}{0.085}\right)$$

$$= P(-2.35 < Z < 3.53) = P(Z < 3.53) - P(Z < -2.53)$$

$$= 0.9998 - 0.0094 = 0.9904.$$

Therefore, the fraction that does not meet the specifications is 1 − 0.9904 = 0.0096.

Approximately 0.96% of components will fall outside specifications for this dimension. [VI.G.2]

96. a; Let X represent the diameter of the steel rod. The upper specification limit is 2.55 and the lower specification limit is 2.45. The proportion of steel rods that are within the specification limits can be written as P(2.45 < X < 2.55). Since the diameter of the steel rod is normally distributed and the process is stable, we can use the standard normal distribution to determine this fraction. From the control charts, an estimate for $\mu$ is $\hat{\mu} = \bar{\bar{x}} = 2.5014$. The point estimate for the process standard deviation is

$$\hat{\sigma} = \frac{\bar{R}}{d_2} = \frac{0.0568}{2.704} = 0.021.$$

The value for $d_2$ can be found in Appendix C of *The Certified Quality Engineer Handbook*, Third Edition for $n = 7$.

Therefore, the fraction of steel rods that meet the specification limits is

$$P(LSL < X < USL) = P(2.45 < X < 2.55) = P\left(\frac{2.45 - 2.5014}{0.021} < \frac{X - \bar{\bar{x}}}{\hat{\sigma}} < \frac{2.55 - 2.5014}{0.021}\right)$$

$$= P(-2.45 < Z < 2.31) = P(Z < 2.31) - P(Z < -2.45)$$

$$= 0.9896 - 0.0071 = 0.9825.$$

Approximately 98.25% of the steel rods will lie within the specification limits. [VI.G.2]

97. d; The specification limits are determined externally, usually by management, engineers, or customers. There is no relationship between the specification limits and control limits. The formula in (a) is the natural limits of a process. The formula in (b) is the control limits of a process. The formula in (c) is the definition of the capability index $C_p$. [VI.G.2]

98. a; USL = 25.85, LSL = 16.85, $\mu$ = 20.98, $\sigma$ = 1.10.

$$C_p = \frac{USL - LSL}{6\sigma} = \frac{25.85 - 16.85}{6(1.10)} = 1.36$$

$$C_{pk} = \min\left\{\frac{USL - \mu}{3\sigma}, \frac{\mu - LSL}{3\sigma}\right\} = \min\left\{\frac{25.85 - 20.98}{3(1.10)}, \frac{20.98 - 16.85}{3(1.10)}\right\}$$

$$= \min\{1.48, 1.25\} = 1.25$$

Since the actual capability, 1.25, is greater than 1.0, we would consider this process capable. [VI.G.3]

99. c; Since the process mean is not centered in the specifications, we use $C_{pk}$ as the measure of capability:

$$C_{pk} = \min\left\{\frac{USL - \mu}{3\sigma}, \frac{\mu - LSL}{3\sigma}\right\} = \min\left\{\frac{19 - 13}{3(1.5)}, \frac{13 - 9}{3(1.5)}\right\} = \min\{1.33, 0.89\} = 0.89.$$

Since $C_{pk} < 1$, the process is not capable. [VI.G.3]

100. a; USL = 2.55, LSL = 2.45, $\bar{\bar{X}} = 2.5014$, $\bar{R} = 0.0568$, $n = 7$

Since the diameter of the steel rod is normally distributed and the process is stable, we can calculate the capability of the process. From the control charts, we can estimate the process standard deviation:

$$\hat{\sigma} = \frac{\bar{R}}{d_2} = \frac{0.0568}{2.704} = 0.021.$$

The value for $d_2$ can be found in Appendix C of *The Certified Quality Engineer Handbook*, Third Edition for $n = 7$. The process is centered in the specifications, so we use $C_p$ as the capability metric.

$$C_p = \frac{USL - LSL}{6\sigma} = \frac{2.55 - 2.45}{6(0.021)} = 0.79$$

Since the capability is less than 1, the process is not considered capable. [VI.G.3]

Part VI
Solutions

101. b; $P_p$ is a performance index that has been recommended for use when the process is not in statistical control. [VI.G.4]

102. c; A treatment combination in experimental design refers to the combination of the levels of each factor assigned to an experimental unit. [VI.H.1]

103. a; The experiment has three factors: temperature, pressure, and time. Each factor is tested at two possible levels. There are four replicates for each treatment combination. [VI.H.1]

104. b; Experimental error is the variation observed in the readings for a particular treatment combination or run. Note that if the number of replications is decreased, the calculation of experimental error is less accurate. [VI.H.1]

105. d; The first step in designing an experiment is to clearly state the objective or goal of the experiment. Defining the goal of the experiment will help with the selection of factors, responses, and measurement method, and selecting the experimental design. [VI.H.2]

106. c; Randomization is the ordering of treatment combinations in a random sequence in order to reduce the effect of unwanted nuisance or noise factors that may influence the results. When the nuisance factors can not be controlled during the experiment, randomizing the treatment combinations will help reduce any effects on the response due to the nuisance variables. Confounding occurs when the effect of one factor is indistinguishable from the effect of another factor or factor interactions. Blocking is used when the nuisance variable can be controlled during the experiment, which eliminates its effect on the response. An interaction is the combined effect of two or more independent factors on the response variable. [VI.H.3]

107. b; Because each experimental run takes several hours and the entire experiment will take place over several days, blocking should be used to eliminate the effect of day. Incorporating the day the experimental run was performed will eliminate any effect that day may have had on the response variable. [VI.H.3]

108. c; When an experiment has a nuisance factor, a blocking factor should be included when carrying out the design and analyzing the results (if possible). We are not interested in determining whether the levels of the blocking factor are significantly different. If we do not include a blocking variable in the experiment, we could reach incorrect conclusions about the factor of interest. [VI.H.4]

109. b; Note that from the ANOVA table, we can determine that there were five levels of factor A and four levels of the blocking variable. The null and alternative hypotheses for this experiment are $H_0 : \tau_1 = \tau_2 = \tau_3 = \tau_4 = \tau_5 = 0$ versus $H_a : \tau_i \neq 0$ for at least one $i$. Since the $p$-value = 0.003 is much smaller than $\alpha = 0.05$, we

reject the null hypothesis and conclude that factor A does have a significant effect on the response. Note that the effect of the blocking variable is not under consideration in the hypothesis test. [VI.H.4]

110. b; Once an experiment has been carried out with a blocking variable, we can not analyze the experiment as if it were not blocked. [VI.H.4]

111. c; There are two factors of interest on the yield. Therefore, there are no blocking factors to consider. A factorial design is appropriate for this experiment. [VI.H.5]

112. b; From the ANOVA table, we test the hypothesis if the main effects and interactions have a significant effect on the response variable. The $p$-value for the main effects of factors A and B is very small (0.000) as is the interaction between factors A and B. The $p$-values of the main effect of factor C and the other interaction terms are large; therefore, we conclude that they do not have a significant effect on the response. [VI.H.5]

113. d; If the order in which the treatments are carried out is known, a run chart of the responses or residuals can help assess the validity of independence. Any noticeable patterns in the run chart indicate lack of independence. [VI.H.5]

114. d; The total degrees of freedom for a design with a single replicate are $2^k - 1$. For $k = 4$, there are $2^4 - 1 = 15$ degrees of freedom available. There are four main effects (A, B, C, and D), six two-way interactions (AB, AC, AD, BC, BD, and CD), four three-way interactions (ABC, ABD, ACD, and BCD), and one four-way interaction (ABCD). This is a total of 15 effects, each with one degree of freedom. Therefore, there are no degrees of freedom left over for error. We can not estimate the process variability in this case. If we were sure that the higher-order interactions were not significant, we could use the sparsity-of-effects principle and pool the degrees of freedom for the higher-order interactions into the error degrees of freedom. [VI.H.5]

115. b; The experiment has $2^{8-1} = 128$ runs. Therefore, the design is a half-fractional factorial design. [VI.H.6]

116. a; In a full-factorial experiment, all main effects and all two-factor interactions are fully estimable. In a fractional factorial experiment, while fewer runs are required, effects are confounded with other effects. [VI.H.6]

117. a; Resolution IV designs have main effects confounded with three-factor or higher interactions, and two-factor interactions confounded with two-factor or higher interactions. With a resolution IV design, we do not know for sure that a two-factor interaction is truly significant or if the two-factor interaction it is aliased with is significant. We may need to add experimental runs to break these aliases. [VI.H.6]

118. c; Using the defining relation $I = ABD = ACE = BCDE$, we can obtain all of the aliases. For factor B, we have:

$$B = B \times I = B \times ABD = AD$$

$$B = B \times I = B \times ACE = ABCE$$

$$B = B \times I = B \times BCDE = CDE$$

Therefore, main effect B is aliased (or confounded) with the two-way interaction AD, the three-way interaction CDE, and the four-way interaction ABCE. [VI.H.6]

119. d; Robustness means resistance to the effect of variation of some factor. The experimenters can control the ingredients (and the amounts) put into the cake mix. They can not control for differences in oven temperatures in their customers' homes. Therefore, the cake mix should be robust to differences in oven temperature. [VI.H.6]

120. b; The control factors in the experiment are the three ingredients. There are two noise, or uncontrollable, factors in the experiment as well: oven temperature and baking time. There is a significant control-by-noise interaction, indicating that one of the controllable variables interacts with the oven temperature. This indicates that it may be possible to find settings of the controllable factors that are robust to variations in the oven temperature. [VI.H.6]

# Part VII
## Risk Management

### (23 Questions)

## QUESTIONS

1. Risk identification is the process of identifying hazards and sources of risks. When an organization is determining possible risks they:

   a. should include only risks that they have control over.

   b. should include only those risks that are obvious and currently known.

   c. should include all possible risks, using many risk identification tools.

   d. should only come up with a list of no more than three to five risks or hazards.

2. The key stakeholders, strategy, and program objectives, as well as development of roles and responsibilities, are typically identified and agreed on in the:

   a. risk management planning.

   b. risk identification phase.

   c. risk prioritization phase.

   d. risk assessment.

3. In a risk analysis, the likelihood and consequences of risk are combined to determine the risk level for a particular risk. The purpose of risk evaluation is to:

   a. make decisions based on risk level compared to stated risk criteria.

   b. determine options for modifying risks.

   c. decide whether risk levels are acceptable.

   d. evaluate and possibly change the consequences.

4. A risk mitigation plan can be used to:

   a. eliminate risk.

   b. minimize risk.

   c.  accept the risk as is.

   d.  All of the above

5.  If the response to a particular risk is to attempt to minimize its impact, this is known as:

   a.  avoidance.

   b.  transfer.

   c.  mitigation.

   d.  denial.

6.  Results of risk evaluation must be:

   a.  quantitative only.

   b.  qualitative only.

   c.  subjective.

   d.  qualitative or quantitative.

7.  The process of comparing the results of a risk analysis that has been completed to the stated risk criteria put in place is:

   a.  risk reduction.

   b.  risk identification.

   c.  risk evaluation.

   d.  None of the above

8.  Risk assessment consists of the following:

   a.  risk identification, analysis, and control.

   b.  risk identification, analysis, and evaluation.

   c.  risk identification, reduction, and evaluation.

   d.  risk reduction, risk criteria, and evaluation.

9.  A risk assessment tool that is based on expert opinion is the:

   a.  checklist.

   b.  Delphi method.

   c.  flowchart.

   d.  FMEA.

10. A failure mode and effects analysis (FMEA) is a useful tool for prioritizing risks. One of the drawbacks or limitations of the FMEA is that:

    a. it can not be used to identify combinations of failure modes, only single failure modes.

    b. it does not aid in identifying possible root causes.

    c. it is too complicated since it does not require the user to know anything about the process or product.

    d. None of the above

11. Two components of risk estimation are:

    a. severity and consequence.

    b. probability of occurrence and severity.

    c. probability of occurrence and risk.

    d. None of the above

12. Qualitative evaluation involves categories such as catastrophic, critical, major, minor, and negligible, which represent:

    a. probabilities of occurrence.

    b. likelihood of occurrence.

    c. severity.

    d. risk priority number.

13. Consider the following table:

|  |  | Probability | | |
|---|---|---|---|---|
|  |  | Low | Medium | High |
| Severity | Low |  |  |  |
|  | Medium |  |  |  |
|  | High |  |  |  |

This table is an example of a(n):

a. flowchart.

b. FMEA.

   c.  severity categorization table.

   d.  risk matrix.

14.  The numerical metric that is an output from an FMEA is the:

   a.  risk priority number.

   b.  significance level.

   c.  capability index.

   d.  supplier index.

15.  Which of the following risk assessment tools is a top-down approach to failure mode analysis?

   a.  FMEA

   b.  FMECA

   c.  FTA

   d.  None of the above

16.  Which of the following is true about hazard and operability (HAZOP) analysis?

   a.  It uses "guide words."

   b.  It is based on the assumption that risks are caused by deviations from the design plans.

   c.  It can be applied to a wide range of processes, products, and services.

   d.  All of the above

17.  The purpose of risk control is to:

   a.  completely eliminate risk.

   b.  completely eliminate all failures.

   c.  maintain risk at or below an acceptable level.

   d.  None of the above

18.  Risk control requires documentation that addresses monitoring and review of risks and controls put in place. Which of the following would not be part of monitoring and review?

   a.  Identifying new or upcoming risks

   b.  Obtaining new information to update risk levels and risk criteria

   c. Assessing the controls in place to make sure they are working and appropriate

   d. All of the above

19. A gap may exist when controlling risks if:

   a. there are controls in place to address significant risks.

   b. there is more than one control in place to address a significant risk.

   c. there is no control in place to address a significant risk or the control is insufficient for that particular risk.

   d. All of the above

20. What activity is performed to verify that known risks are being controlled and that risk treatment plans in place are effective?

   a. Risk reduction

   b. Risk audit

   c. Risk control

   d. Risk reporting

21. Residual risk is:

   a. risk that remains after a risk treatment has been implemented.

   b. risk due to a gap between what is believed to be risk and what really is risk.

   c. unknown risk that can never be identified.

   d. None of the above

22. Risk reduction and risk acceptance are the two components of:

   a. risk control.

   b. risk audit.

   c. residual risk.

   d. risk reporting.

23. Controls and risks should be monitored to determine whether:

   a. risk assessment techniques are being appropriately implemented.

   b. expected results of the risk management process are being maintained.

   c. risk treatments in place are still effective.

   d. All of the above

# SOLUTIONS

1. c; The purpose of risk identification is to identify all possible risks whether current, possible future risks, risks that are not currently under the organization's control, or risks that may occur due to results of an accumulation of factors or steps in the process. [VII.A.1]

2. a; The planning phase is important for setting all ground rules and objectives, and identifying key stakeholders. It may also include selecting key documents and templates for risk analysis. [VII.A.1]

3. a; Risk evaluation is used to make decisions about which risks need to be addressed based on the estimate of metrics identified in risk analysis—combined results of the likelihood of the risk and the consequences. [VII.A.2]

4. d; A risk mitigation plan is implemented once risks have been identified. They then must be evaluated to determine whether the risk is worth eliminating or minimizing, or to accept the risk and do nothing about it. [VII.A.3]

5. c; Risk mitigation includes the act of attempting to minimize the risk's impact on the system, process, or product. [VII.A.3]

6. d; Once a risk analysis has been performed, the final evaluation of the results may be quantitative or qualitative, or both. [VII.A.2]

7. c; Risk evaluation; once estimates of the evaluation metrics have been calculated, they should be compared to the level of risk or risk criteria already in place to determine whether the level of risk is acceptable. [VII.B]

8. b; The three components of risk assessment are risk identification, risk analysis, and risk evaluation. [VII.B]

9. b; The Delphi method is based on the idea that group decisions or judgments will be more accurate than those of individuals. [VII.B]

10. a; The FMEA can not identify combinations of failure modes, and failure mode combinations may be significant. [VII.B]

11. b; The two components for risk estimation include the probability of occurrence of harm and the severity or potential harm. [VII.B]

12. c; The qualitative assessment where the degree of risk or harm is given as catastrophic, critical, and so on, represents the severity or potential harm. [VII.B]

13. d; The table represents a risk matrix (also known as a risk assessment matrix). It contains information on the probability of a certain level of risk and the level of severity. [VII.B]

14. a; The risk priority number is a numerical result from the FMEA. The RPN is the result of multiplying three values: severity of failure, failure likelihood, and the likelihood of detecting the failure. [VII.B]

15. c; FMEA and FMECA are both bottom-up approaches, while fault tree analysis (FTA) is a top-down approach. [VII.B]

16. d; HAZOP can be used to identify operability issues and potential hazards that may lead to unacceptable products, processes, or services. [VII.B]

17. c; The main goal of risk control is to maintain the level risk at an acceptably low level. [VII.C.1]

18. d; Each of the choices are some of the information that should be included in any risk control documentation. [VII.C.1]

19. c; A gap occurs when the control in place is not adequate for the risk, or no control has been put in place for a significant risk. Answer (b) is called a redundancy. [VII.C.1]

20. b; In addition to determining whether known risks are being controlled and risk treatment plans are effective, risk audits can be helpful in identifying new risks. [VII.C.2]

21. a; Residual risk is that risk remaining even after a treatment of a known risk has been implemented. There are times when a risk treatment does not eliminate a risk but only minimizes it until the risk is at or below an acceptable level. [VII.C.1]

22. a; Risk reduction focuses on the avoidance of risk, while risk acceptance focuses on the decision to accept risk. Together, they are risk control. [VII.C.1]

23. d; These are just some of the goals of monitoring a risk management process. Others include determining whether assumptions made previously when estimating risk are still valid, and whether risk assessment results match or mirror actual results. [VII.C.2]

# Section 2
## Additional Practice Problems

Section 2 contains 205 additional practice problems. These questions represent material from each of the seven parts in the *Certified Quality Engineer* Body of Knowledge. The questions are in a randomized order. Detailed solutions can be found in a section at the end of all the questions.

## QUESTIONS

1. Which of the following is a disadvantage of pre-control charts?

    a. They do not provide information on how to reduce variability in a process.

    b. They can not determine if a product being produced is centered between the tolerances during initial operation setup.

    c. They are difficult to interpret.

    d. They can be used for processes with a capability ratio less than 1.

2. In a gage R&R study, the standard deviation associated with repeatability was found to be 0.9214, and the standard deviation associated with reproducibility was found to be 0.5873. What is the standard deviation associated with measurement error?

    a. 1.1939

    b. 1.0927

    c. 1.5087

    d. None of the above

3. Which of the following is considered attribute data?

    a. Customer wait time

    b. Number of filing errors

    c. Costs of processing applications

    d. Thickness of a component

4. True/False. In a series system, the failure of one subsystem results in the failure of the entire system.

    a. True

    b. False

5. A system improvement program based on minimizing variability is called:

    a. Lean Six Sigma.

    b. Six Sigma.

    c. lean.

    d. theory of constraints.

6. A population has a distribution with mean 24 and standard deviation 5.5. What is the approximate standard deviation of the sampling distribution of the sample mean if random samples of size 32 are taken?

   a.  5.5

   b.  5.5/32

   c.  $5.5/\sqrt{24}$

   d.  $5.5/\sqrt{32}$

7. Which of the following involves verifying that the process parameters in place will result in a product or process that meets all requirements under all possible manufacturing conditions?

   a.  Installation qualification

   b.  Operational qualification

   c.  Performance qualification

   d.  Software qualification

8. Last month, a local company reported the following quality costs:

   | | |
   |---|---|
   | Incoming inspection | $ 60,000 |
   | Design support | $ 12,000 |
   | Field trials | $110,000 |
   | Returns by customers | $ 40,000 |

   What is the total appraisal cost for last month?

   a.  $60,000

   b.  $72,000

   c.  $170,000

   d.  $65,000

9. A control chart monitoring the viscosity of a product shows that a particular process is out of control. What should the process operator do?

   a.  Attempt to fix the problem on their own.

   b.  Follow the reaction plan detailed in the control plan of the process.

   c.  Brainstorm to determine the cause of the problem.

   d.  Nothing; the process will stabilize on its own.

10.  An $\bar{X}$ and $R$ chart was prepared for an operation using 25 samples with four pieces in each sample. $\bar{\bar{X}}$ was found to be 26.75 and $\bar{R}$ was 8.10. During production, a sample of four was taken and the pieces measured 20, 29, 40, and 25. At the time this sample was taken:

   a.  both the average and range were within the control limits.

   b.  neither the average nor range were within the control limits.

   c.  only the average was outside the control limits.

   d.  only the range was outside the control limits.

11.  In the third region identified in a bathtub curve, what is the most common cause for failures?

   a.  The manufacturing process

   b.  Wear-out

   c.  Random failures

   d.  None of the above

12.  Performance measures:

   a.  do not need to be achievable.

   b.  do not need to be measurable.

   c.  should be linked to strategic objectives.

   d.  should focus on as many measures as possible.

13.  What is the main purpose of an interrelationship digraph?

   a.  To organize and summarize ideas generated about a particular problem or issue

   b.  To communicate hierarchical relationships between events

   c.  To assess a process implementation plan during the initial phases of operations

   d.  To visualize and identify causal relationships of a problem or situation

14. A defect was discovered in a laptop battery. How should the company handle the disposition of this defective battery?

    a.  Immediately scrap all defective batteries

    b.  Wait for the decision of the material review board (MRB)

    c.  Begin a product traceability flowchart

    d.  Continue production as usual

15. Suppose that the *p*-value of a hypothesis test on $\mu_1 - \mu_2$ is 0.23. What conclusions can be made (use significance level 10%)?

    a.  Reject $H_0$, conclude that the two means are the same.

    b.  Reject $H_0$, conclude that the two means are not the same.

    c.  Do not reject $H_0$, conclude that the two means are the same.

    d.  Do not reject $H_0$, conclude that the two means are not the same.

16. What is the maximum possible value of an RPN?

    a.  10

    b.  1

    c.  100

    d.  None of the above

17. Teams that are formed for the purpose of improving an existing process or developing a new one are:

    a.  self-directed work teams.

    b.  work groups.

    c.  process improvement teams.

    d.  All of the above

18. A part was inspected using a go/no-go gage. The part mated with both ends of the gage. Did the part pass inspection?

    a.  No, the part should be rejected.

    b.  Yes, the part should be accepted.

    c.  Not enough information provided

19. What quality tool would be good for conducting a needs analysis when considering a new training program?

    a. Checklists

    b. Histogram

    c. QFD

    d. Control chart

20. Which phase of the corrective action cycle helps prevent problem backsliding?

    a. Problem identification

    b. Correction

    c. Recurrence control

    d. Effectiveness assessment

21. A team measured the time to failure of 20 components. They plotted the data in a Weibull probability plot, shown below. What conclusions can be drawn from this plot?

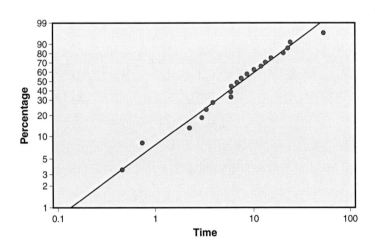

    a. The normal distribution is not a reasonable model for the time to failure.

    b. The Weibull distribution is a reasonable model for the time to failure.

    c. The normal distribution is a reasonable model for the time to failure.

    d. Not enough information is provided to draw conclusions.

22. A team investigated the number of patient falls in a hospital. 56 patients were randomly selected. Out of the 56 patients, there were six recorded patient falls. Using this information, construct a 90% confidence interval on the true proportion of patient falls in this hospital.

    a.  (−0.4016, 0.6158)

    b.  (0, 0.6158)

    c.  (0.0006, 0.2136)

    d.  (0.0391, 0.1751)

23. A gage R&R study was performed for a process with 10 parts, two operators, and three replicates. The $\bar{X}$ chart below displays information about the gage capability. What conclusions can be drawn from this control chart?

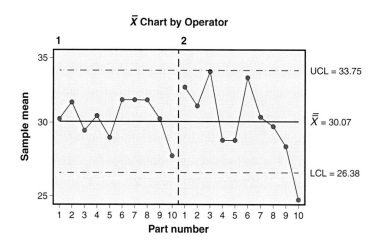

    a.  The gage is capable of distinguishing between parts.

    b.  There is a significant difference between operators.

    c.  The chart reflects variability related to gage reproducibility.

    d.  The gage is not capable of distinguishing between parts.

24. Consider the product/process development life cycle. The phase in which a working model of the product or process is developed and tested is referred to as the:

    a.  prototype phase.

    b.  production phase.

    c.  concept phase.

    d.  specification phase.

25. Find the probability that Z, the standard normal distribution, lies between –1.02 and 0.58.

    a.  0.5651

    b.  0.1539

    c.  0.7190

    d.  0.4349

26. A lot of size 100 is to be inspected using ANSI/ASQ Z1.4-2003 (R2013). The AQL is 1.5%. What is the required sample size for a single sampling plan (normal, level II inspection)?

    a.  5

    b.  13

    c.  32

    d.  None of the above

27. The reliability function of a television is defined as $R(t) = 998/1000$. What is the probability that a randomly selected television from the population fails by time $t$?

    a.  998/1000

    b.  0

    c.  2/1000

    d.  None of the above

28. Which quality leader proposed using signal-to-noise ratios to improve robustness of a process?

    a.  Deming

    b.  Taguchi

    c.  Juran

    d.  Ishikawa

29. The date of a customer's visit to a store is on which measurement scale?

    a.  Nominal

    b.  Ordinal

    c.  Interval

    d.  Ratio

30. What is a benefit of implementing standardized work in an organization?

    a.  Reductions in process variation

    b.  More consistent products

    c.  Simplified downstream activities

    d.  All of the above

31. A sequential sampling plan has an accept line defined as Accept line = $0.1043n - 1.2486$. For a sample size $n = 35$, what is the acceptance number?

    a.  1

    b.  2

    c.  3

    d.  None of the above

32. A control chart was out of control, but the operator failed to adjust the process. What is this called?

    a.  Common cause variation

    b.  Special cause variation

    c.  Overcontrol

    d.  Undercontrol

33. A new app released for cell phones occasionally crashes during customer use. How would the app's developing company classify this defect?

    a.  Minor defect

    b.  Major defect

    c.  Serious defect

    d.  Critical defect

34. A $3^5$ experiment means that we are investigating:

    a.  three levels of five factors.

    b.  three independent variables and five replicates.

    c.  five levels of three factors.

    d.  five independent variables and three response variables.

35. A company is deciding between two competing sampling plans for a product they receive from a manufacturer. The diagram below displays the operating characteristic (OC) curves for these two sampling plans.

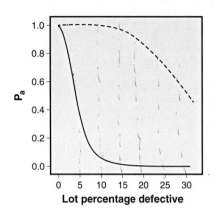

Compared to the solid line, the dashed OC curve:

a.  is better for the company.

b.  is better for the manufacturer.

c.  has a low probability of accepting lots with poor quality.

d.  None of the above

36. The failure rate of a machine is 0.0008. Assuming the life distribution of this type of machine is exponential, what is the probability that a randomly selected machine will fail by the mean time to failure?

a.  0.3679

b.  0.6321

c.  1250

d.  0.9992

37. The side-by-side box plots below show the wait times of customers at two grocery stores. What can be said about these wait times?

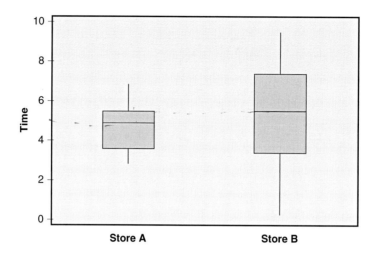

a. The wait times at store A are more variable than those at store B.

b. The distribution of wait times at both stores is not bell shaped.

c. The wait times at store B are more variable than those at store A.

d. Customers at store A tend to wait longer than those at store B.

38. A two-way ANOVA was used to test the effects of two factors on a response variable. What conclusions can be drawn from the interaction plot below?

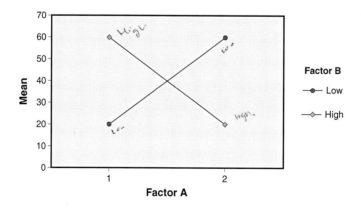

a. High levels of factor B tend to have smaller response values.

b. There is not an interaction effect between factors A and B.

c. There is an interaction effect between factors A and B.

d. Factors A and B do not have an effect on the response variable.

39. Our company wants to begin rating the capabilities of one of our new suppliers. The process for rating this supplier must include:

    a. rating the supplier's physical location.

    b. rating the supplier's employees' ethnicity because we only want a certain ethnicity working for our suppliers.

    c. rating the supplier's financial, manufacturing, and quality systems.

    d. All of the above

40. A quality project team is investigating the root cause of variation in a fish tank manufacturing facility. In what stage of the DMAIC process is this team?

    a. D

    b. M

    c. A

    d. I

    e. C

41. Consider a sampling plan with $n = 80$ and $c = 2$. Given that the percentage nonconforming is 0.025 and a Poisson distribution is appropriate, what is the probability of accepting the lot?

    a. 0.677

    b. 0.323

    c. 0.406

    d. 0.857

42. Tensile strength of cement is of interest to a company. Historical studies indicate that tensile strength is normally distributed and that the standard deviation of tensile strength is 1.25 psi. A random sample of 15 cement pieces had a mean tensile strength of 124 psi. The company would like to determine if the mean tensile strength is more than 120 psi at the 5% significance level. What is the test statistic for this hypothesis test?

    a. 1.645

    b. 12.39

    c. –12.39

    d. 1.96

43. The MTTF for a machine is 525 hours. What fraction of machines fail by 1000 hours? Assume the reliability of the machine has an exponential distribution.

    a.  85.11%

    b.  14.89%

    c.  0.19%

    d.  99.81%

44. Which of the following components of measurement systems contributes to the precision?

    a.  Bias

    b.  Linearity

    c.  Stability

    d.  Reproducibility

45. A team suspects that there is a linear relationship between two continuous variables. What is the first thing they should do when examining the relationship between these two variables?

    a.  Calculate the correlation coefficient

    b.  Fit a linear regression model of the two variables

    c.  Graph the data in a scatter diagram

    d.  Compare histograms of the two variables

46. If the probability that event A occurs is 0.62, the probability that event B occurs is 0.09, and events A and B are statistically independent, what is the probability that event A and B both occur?

    a.  0.0558

    b.  0.71

    c.  0.53

    d.  Not enough information provided

47. A system improvement program based on eliminating waste is called:

    a.  Lean Six Sigma.

    b.  Six Sigma.

  c. lean.

  d. theory of constraints.

48. In which phase of the corrective action cycle does a team develop feasible solutions to improve a process?

  a. Problem identification

  b. Correction

  c. Recurrence control

  d. Effectiveness assessment

49. Measurement assurance is an important concept in metrology because:

  a. calibration of measuring equipment is critical.

  b. consistent measuring devices provide confidence in the accuracy of the process.

  c. little consideration is often given to a test operator's contribution to measurement error.

  d. random errors in measurement must be taken into account.

50. When there is no control in place to address a significant risk, or the control is insufficient for that particular risk, there is a

  a. control gap.

  b. risk reduction.

  c. missed risk.

  d. All of the above

51. An experiment is being conducted on the yield of a substance. Two factors are believed to have an effect on the yield. The experiment will take place over several days. What type of design would be appropriate for this experiment?

  a. Interaction

  b. Randomized block design

  c. Factorial design

  d. Half-fractional factorial design

52. True/False. The most readable measuring equipment always leads to the most accurate measurements.

    a. True

    b. False

53. A normally distributed process has specifications $20.35 \pm 3.50$. $\bar{X}$ and $R$ control charts (based on samples of size four) indicate there is an out-of-control point. The control charts also indicate that $\bar{\bar{X}} = 20.98$ and $\bar{R} = 1.96$. What is the process capability?

    a. 1.23

    b. 1.01

    c. 1.45

    d. Unknown

54. The scatter plot below displays a relationship between two variables. What is the correlation coefficient of these two variables?

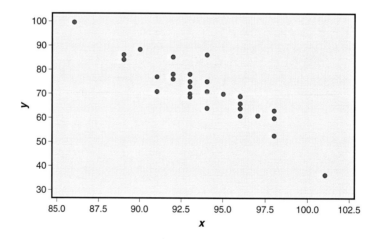

    a. 0.90

    b. 0

    c. −1.82

    d. −0.90

55. Evaluation of the capability of equipment, selection of measurement standards, and detailed procedures to carry out measurements are key components of:

    a. gage R&R studies.

b.  sampling plans.

c.  poka-yoke.

d.  calibration control systems.

56. Which of the following statements best describes the hazard rate function $h(t)$?

a.  It is a measure of the instantaneous rate of failure of a component at time $t$.

b.  It is the probability that a component will survive past time $t$.

c.  It is the fraction of all components in the population that survive past time $t$.

d.  It is the average number of failures through time $t$.

57. A team would like to estimate the true average tensile strength of cement. They would like to obtain an estimate within 0.05 MPa of the true average tensile strength with 99% confidence. Based on prior information, it is assumed that $\sigma = 0.50$ MPa. What sample size is required to meet these requirements?

a.  663

b.  664

c.  25

d.  26

58. How is risk assessed in an FMEA?

a.  The likelihood of a failure occurring

b.  The likelihood of detecting a failure once it has occurred

c.  The severity of a failure if it occurs

d.  All of the above

59. The inside dimensions of a part are inspected for conformance to product specifications. Which of the following measuring tools is most appropriate to inspect its dimensions?

a.  Spline

b.  Ring gage

c.  Plug gage

d.  Micrometer

60. A factory collected data on the number of nonconforming parts to construct an *np*-chart. 15 samples of size 150 were collected. They determined that the average fraction nonconforming was $\bar{p} = 0.045$. During production, a sample of 150 parts was taken, of which 18 were nonconforming. At the time this sample was taken:

    a. the sample was within the control limits.

    b. the sample was outside the control limits.

    c. the upper control limit was 0.12.

    d. the lower control limit was 0.

61. What is the effect of a factor that is indistinguishable from the effect of the interaction of two other factors called?

    a. Randomization

    b. Replication

    c. Confounding

    d. Efficiency

62. A company produces a part continuously. Which type of OC curve is appropriate for the proposed sampling plan?

    a. Type A OC curve

    b. Type B OC curve

    c. Normal OC curve

    d. None of the above

63. Consider the following *c*-chart. What conclusions can be drawn from this control chart?

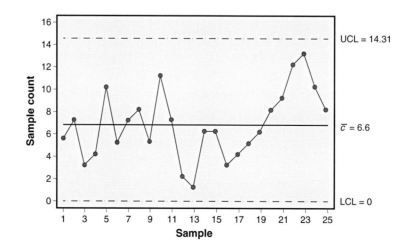

   a. The process is out of control.

   b. The process is stable.

   c. The process is operating within the specifications.

   d. The process is operating outside the specifications.

64. In a gage R&R study, the variance associated with repeatability was found to be 0.8842, and the variance associated with reproducibility was found to be 0.2466. What is the total process variance?

   a. 0.6376

   b. 1.4369

   c. 1.1308

   d. Not enough information provided

65. Which of the following probability distributions is right-skewed?

   a. Lognormal

   b. Exponential

   c. Chi-square

   d. All of the above

66. A company maintained a large stock of supplies in their warehouse. As a result, a sizeable portion of the materials had degraded by the time that they were required. As what type of waste would the company classify this event?

   a. Inventory

   b. Waiting

   c. Overproduction

   d. Excess processing

67. Which of the following can you typically find in a reaction plan for a process?

   a. A detailed description of the process

   b. The machine number used in the process

   c. Normal probability plots

   d. Steps for appropriate disposition of suspect material/products

68. A team wants to predict a person's cholesterol based on their weight in pounds. The fitted regression equation is Cholesterol = 135 + 0.28 × Weight. What is the predicted cholesterol of a person who weighs 175 pounds?

    a. 184

    b. 135

    c. 0.28

    d. 212.80

69. Common development stages that teams often progress through are known as *forming, storming, norming,* and *performing.* In the "norming" stage:

    a. individuals begin to shift from personal concerns to the needs of the team.

    b. the team's mission is clarified and specific roles are identified.

    c. team members still think and act as individuals instead of impacting as a team.

    d. the team has matured and is working in the best interest of the team and team goals.

70. In acceptance sampling, what does the acronym "AOQ" mean?

    a. The quality level

    b. The poorest quality in an individual lot that should be accepted

    c. The average quality of outgoing products

    d. The worst tolerable process average of a continuing series of lots

71. A company is releasing a new computer and is developing a traceability flowchart. Which of the following components should be included in this flowchart?

    a. A list of the critical parts in the computer

    b. Each part's vendor

    c. Detailed shipping records

    d. All of the above

72. A machine has three identical and independent subsystems, each with a reliability of 0.95. The system design requires that a minimum of two subsystems must function for the system to operate. What is the system reliability of this machine?

   a.  0.9928

   b.  0.9025

   c.  0.9999

   d.  0.8574

73. In a crossed-array designed experiment, it is found that there are no significant control-by-noise interactions. This means that:

   a.  it may be possible to find settings of the controllable variables that are robust to the noise factors.

   b.  there is high experimental error.

   c.  there is no robust design problem.

   d.  the controllable factors have no effect on the response.

74. In an acceptance sampling plan, how does the probability of acceptance change for a given fraction nonconforming as the acceptance number increases? Assume that the sample size and lot size are held constant.

   a.  $P_a$ increases.

   b.  $P_a$ decreases.

   c.  $P_a$ stays constant.

   d.  Not enough information provided

75. A hypothesis test on the variance of the wait times of customers at a store was conducted. You would like to determine if the variance of the wait time is less than 4 minutes$^2$. A random sample of 22 wait times had a variance of 1.75 minutes$^2$. At the 5% significance level, what is your conclusion from this hypothesis test?

   a.  Reject $H_0$, conclude that the variance equals 4 minutes$^2$.

   b.  Reject $H_0$, conclude that the variance is less than 4 minutes$^2$.

   c.  Do not reject $H_0$, conclude that the variance equals 4 minutes$^2$.

   d.  Do not reject $H_0$, conclude that the variance is less than 4 minutes$^2$.

76. Accounting for a $1.5\sigma$ shift in the mean of a process, how many defective parts per million are produced for a process operating at $6\sigma$ quality?

    a. 3.4

    b. 0.002

    c. 2700

    d. None of the above

77. Suppose an experiment has four factors A, B, C, and D, with four, two, three, and two levels investigated, respectively. How many treatment combinations are in a full-factorial experimental design for these factors?

    a. 4

    b. 48

    c. 16

    d. 11

78. A manufacturer produces a particular part that is complex. Which of the following measurement tools is most appropriate to inspect its dimensions?

    a. Precision spindle

    b. Coordinate measuring machine

    c. Micrometer calipers

    d. Go/no-go gage

79. Twenty-eight failures occurred after 750 machines were tested for five hours. What is the mean time to failure for these machines, assuming the reliability of this machine has an exponential distribution?

    a. 133

    b. 0.037

    c. 27

    d. 0.0075

80. Type II error in hypothesis testing corresponds to which of the following in acceptance sampling?

    a. Consumer's risk

    b. Producer's risk

81. A certain computer company will not build their final product until a customer supplies them with all their desired options. What type of system does this company use?

    a. Pull system

    b. Push system

    c. 5S

    d. Six Sigma

82. Consider the contingency table presented below. A hypothesis test for independence is conducted to determine whether the number of nonconforming parts produced is independent of time of day.

| Time | Conforming parts | Nonconforming parts | Totals |
|---|---|---|---|
| Day | 82 | 18 | 100 |
| Evening | 75 | 19 | 94 |
| Overnight | 45 | 14 | 59 |
| Totals | 202 | 51 | 253 |

The value of the test statistic for this hypothesis test is 0.757. At the 10% significance level, what is the conclusion from this hypothesis test?

    a. Reject $H_0$, conclude that type of parts produced and time of day are independent.

    b. Reject $H_0$, conclude that type of parts produced and time of day are not independent.

    c. Do not reject $H_0$, conclude that type of parts produced and time of day are independent.

    d. Do not reject $H_0$, conclude that type of parts produced and time of day are not independent.

83. The failure rate of a machine is 0.0008. Assuming the life distribution of this type of repairable machine is exponential and the MTTR is 48 hours, what is the steady-state availability of this machine?

    a. 1298

    b. 0.963

c. 0.037

d. 1250

84. A company's shipment of textbooks to customers became illegible during the printing process due to an ink malfunction. The company must replace each customer's order. How would the company classify this defect?

   a. Minor defect

   b. Major defect

   c. Serious defect

   d. Critical defect

85. A population has a distribution that is highly right-skewed. One hundred samples of size eight are randomly collected, and the 100 sample means are calculated. What is the approximate distribution of these sample averages?

   a. Normal

   b. Binomial

   c. Uniform

   d. None of the above

86. The number of defects on a TV screen is being examined. Thirty-two TV screens are randomly chosen each day over a 22-day period and examined for defects. The average number of defects is $\bar{c} = 5.68$. What is the upper control limit for a corresponding $c$-chart?

   a. 12.83

   b. 6.94

   c. 0

   d. 22.65

87. What is the recommended first step to take when prioritizing corrective action?

   a. Eliminate occurrence

   b. Eliminate severity

   c. Improve detection

   d. None of the above

88. To get more accurate measurements, which of the following is recommended?

    a. Granite surface plate

    b. Iron surface plate

    c. Steel ruler

    d. None of the above

89. Is inspection considered a value-added or non-value-added activity?

    a. Value-added

    b. Non-value-added

    c. It depends

90. Consider the four layers or tiers of a quality manual. Which layer describes the company's commitments, what it stands for, and objectives for quality?

    a. First layer/tier: policy statement

    b. Second layer/tier: procedures

    c. Third layer/tier: work instructions

    d. Fourth layer/tier: quality records/results of implementation

91. The voltage of a power supply is of interest to a team. Voltage is assumed to be normally distributed. The voltages of nine randomly selected observations are: 9.66, 8.25, 12.46, 12.35, 11.52, 8.92, 11.00, 11.12, and 11.13. Find the 99% confidence interval on the population standard deviation of the voltage.

    a. (0.783, 12.792)

    b. (0.885, 3.577)

    c. (9.072, 12.325)

    d. (0.534, 8.726)

92. Consider the following $\bar{X}$ chart from a normally distributed process. What conclusions can be drawn from this control chart?

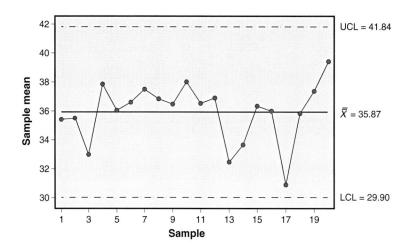

a. The process is out of control.

b. The process is stable.

c. The process is operating within the specifications.

d. The process is operating outside the specifications.

93. The fitted regression equation for two variables $x$ and $y$ is $\hat{y} = -7.5x - 19$. What is the intercept of this line?

a. 7.5

b. 19

c. -7.5

d. -19

94. A manufacturer would like to detect surface defects in a particular part. The surface of this part is made of aluminum. Which of the following testing methods is most appropriate?

a. Liquid penetration testing

b. Magnetic particle testing

c. 100% inspection

d. Coordinate measuring machine

95. Which of the following terms describes the phenomenon in which high-order interactions are negligible and a system is dominated by the main effects and low-order interactions?

    a.  Homogeneity of variance

    b.  Central limit theorem

    c.  Sparsity-of-effects principle

    d.  Independence

96. If the probability that event A occurs is 0.40, the probability that event B occurs is 0.13, and A and B are mutually exclusive, what is the probability that either A or B occurs?

    a.  0.53

    b.  0.052

    c.  1.53

    d.  0

97. A hypothesis test is performed at the 5% significance level. The probability of a type II error of the test is 0.15. What is the power for this hypothesis test?

    a.  0.95

    b.  0.85

    c.  0.05

    d.  0.15

98. The scatter plot below displays the relationship between two random variables. What is the correlation coefficient of these two variables?

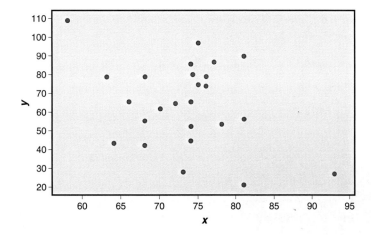

a.  –0.39

b.  –0.91

c.  0.39

d.  0.91

99. The calibration of a measuring standard for a machine has become faulty. This is an example of:

a.  random error in measurement.

b.  systematic error in measurement.

c.  type I error.

d.  type II error.

100. A specification is given as $10^{+0.002/-0.000}$. The limits for this specification are:

a.  10.000 and 10.002

b.  9.998 and 10.000

c.  9.998 and 10.002

d.  10.000

101. The waiting times in minutes for eight customers at a bank are: 5, 8, 12, 3, 2, 7, 6, and 5. What is the mode for this sample of waiting times?

a.  5.5 minutes

b.  6 minutes

c.  5 minutes

d.  3.12 minutes

102. The reliability function at time $t$ for a lawnmower is $R(t) = 4890/5000$. Which of the following statements is true?

a.  The probability that a random lawnmower will survive for a time less than $t$ is $4890/5000$.

b.  $4890/5000$ of all lawnmowers in the population fail by time $t$.

c.  The probability that a randomly selected lawnmower fails by time $t$ is $4890/5000$.

d.  The probability that a randomly selected lawnmower will survive for a time greater than $t$ is $4890/5000$.

103. The dimension of a component has specifications of $10.80 \pm 2.50$. The process data are normally distributed with mean 10.45 and standard deviation 1.05. Find the actual capability of this process.

    a.  0.90

    b.  0.79

    c.  1.27

    d.  0.68

104. Philip Crosby is credited with which definition of quality?

    a.  Fitness for use

    b.  Conformance to specification

    c.  Defect-free products

    d.  Uniformity around a target value

105. A team at a hospital did a project on medication errors. A random sample of medication errors yielded the following results:

| Type of error | Number of errors |
|---|---|
| Incorrect dose | 22 |
| Wrong dose | 34 |
| Incorrect form | 47 |
| Wrong amount | 45 |
| Total | 148 |

The team used a goodness-of-fit test to determine whether the medication errors occur with equal probabilities. The test statistic was 10.757. At the 5% significance level, what is the conclusion from this hypothesis test?

    a.  Reject $H_0$, conclude that the medication errors occur with the same probability.

    b.  Reject $H_0$, conclude that the medication errors do not occur with the same probability.

    c.  Do not reject $H_0$, conclude that the medication errors occur with the same probability.

    d.  Do not reject $H_0$, conclude that the medication errors do not occur with the same probability.

106. In what way does the official definition of the base unit of mass differ from the definitions of other base units?

    a. Its definition has been changed several times by the International Bureau of Weights and Measures.

    b. Its definition is based on the speed of light.

    c. Its definition is in terms of a physical artifact.

    d. None of the above

107. If a process is out of control, it is desirable to:

    a. not adjust the process.

    b. have a small average run length.

    c. have a large average run length.

    d. stop monitoring the process.

108. Which of the following graphical tools can be used to find the optimal settings of factors in a factorial experiment?

    a. Histogram

    b. Normal probability plot

    c. Contour plot

    d. Scatter plot

109. A sequential sampling plan has the following parameters: $\alpha = 0.01$, AQL = 0.025, $\beta = 0.10$, RQL = 0.15. Which of the following statements about this sampling plan is true?

    a. The plan has a 1% chance of rejecting a lot that is 2.5% defective.

    b. The plan has a 1% chance of accepting a lot that is 2.5% defective.

    c. The plan has a 15% chance of accepting a lot that is 2.5% defective.

    d. The plan has a 15% chance of rejecting a lot that is 15% defective.

110. A bottling company's filling process has a normal distribution with mean 24 oz and standard deviation 0.05 oz. What is the probability that a sample of nine randomly selected bottles will have an average volume less than 23.96 oz?

    a. 0

    b. 0.2119

c.  0.9918

d.  0.0082

111.  Which of the following is *not* an objective of statistical process control (SPC)?

a.  SPC shows whether process variation appears to be random.

b.  SPC helps determine whether a process is improving.

c.  SPC indicates when a process has nonrandom variation.

d.  SPC tells you what caused out-of-control behavior in a process.

112.  A certain part has a target length of 5.00 cm. The length of the same type of part was repeatedly measured 10 times at three points in time over a two-month period. On day one, the observed average was 5.007; after one month, the observed average was 4.975; after two months, the observed average was 4.824. Which of the following statements is true?

a.  There is evidence of nonlinearity in this measurement system.

b.  There is evidence of stability issues in this measurement system.

c.  The measurement system is not reproducible.

d.  The measurement system is not repeatable.

113.  Which of the following probability distributions is often used to model the first region of the general failure rate model (the bathtub curve)?

a.  Uniform

b.  Exponential

c.  Normal

d.  Weibull

114.  Consider the following system where the reliability of each component is displayed within each box. What is the reliability of the overall system?

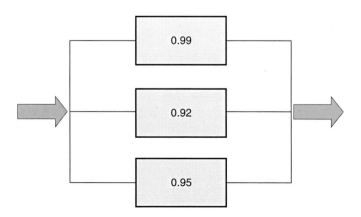

a. 0.8653

b. 0.9999

c. 0.95

d. None of the above

115. An online ordering form for a company will not go through unless the customer has completely filled out all the shipping information and their address is automatically checked as a valid address. This is an example of:

a. Poka-yoke

b. Kanban

c. 5S

d. Robust design

116. A quantity derived from sample data that describes the distribution is called a:

a. parameter.

b. statistic.

c. population.

d. critical value.

117. A disadvantage of using a fractional factorial experiment is that:

a. it requires more runs.

b. it is more difficult to analyze.

c. measurements are less accurate.

d. effects are confounded.

118. True/False. If the failure rate of a system is constant, a preventive maintenance policy is recommended.

a. True

b. False

119. The probability of correctly rejecting a false null hypothesis is called:

a. power.

b. type I error.

c. type II error.

d. significance level.

120. The scatter plot below displays the relationship between two random variables. What is the correlation coefficient of these two variables?

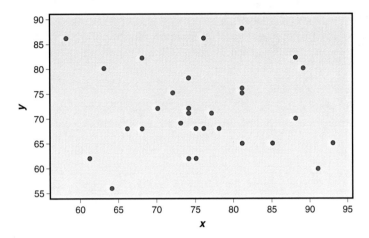

   a. 0.93

   b. –0.93

   c. 0

   d. 1.62

121. A lot size of 50,000 is to be inspected using ANSI/ASQ Z1.4-2003 (R2013). The AQL is 1.0%. What are the required sample size, acceptance number, and rejection number for a single sampling plan (normal, level II inspection)?

   a. $n = 500$, Ac = 10, Re = 11

   b. $n = 500$, Ac = 7, Re = 8

   c. $n = 800$, Ac = 14, Re = 15

   d. $n = 800$, Ac = 10, Re = 11

122. A factory has historically produced defective parts 1% of the time. Samples of 50 independent parts produced in the factory are tested for the presence or absence of a defect. The resulting data (the number of parts that are defective) form which type of distribution?

   a. Poisson

   b. Hypergeometric

   c. Normal

   d. Binomial

123. The diameter of a stainless steel rod is an important quality characteristic. The rod has specifications 1.50 ± 0.08. Data from the process indicate that the distribution is normally distributed, and $\bar{X}$ and $R$ charts indicate that the process is stable. The control charts used a sample of size four and found that $\bar{X}$ =1.4983 and $\bar{R}$ = 0.0906. What fraction of steel rods will fall outside the specification limits?

    a.  0.9311

    b.  0.0689

    c.  0.0375

    d.  0.9686

124. What is the function of a tree diagram?

    a.  To discover a hierarchical relationship between events that led to a failure in a process

    b.  To map out the events that lead to a particular outcome

    c.  To develop alternate concepts to meet a desired requirement

    d.  All of the above

125. The attribute sampling plan for a specific product utilizes an accept value of 3 and reject value of 7. The inspector discovers six defective items in the current sample. What is the next appropriate action?

    a.  Accept the lot since the number of defective items is less than the Re value.

    b.  Reject the lot since the number of defective items is more than the Ac value.

    c.  Draw another sample.

    d.  None of the above

126. Active listening by team members is an important skill that is not often easy to attain with new teams. There are several dimensions to active listening. Which of the following is *not* one of the dimensions of active listening?

    a.  Listening to understand

    b.  Confirming

    c.  Clarifying

    d.  Being defensive

127. The distribution on which *np*-charts are based is called:

    a.  Poisson.

    b.  binomial.

    c.  normal.

    d.  exponential.

128. Consider the contingency table presented below. Given a nonconforming part, what is the probability it was made during the day shift?

| Time | Conforming parts | Nonconforming parts | Totals |
|---|---|---|---|
| Day | 94 | 5 | 99 |
| Evening | 87 | 10 | 97 |
| Overnight | 65 | 23 | 88 |
| Totals | 246 | 38 | 284 |

    a.  0.05

    b.  0.13

    c.  0.38

    d.  0.02

129. A random sample of eight pieces of plastic tubing is selected. The inside diameter of the tubing is known to be normally distributed. The inside diameters of the eight pieces of plastic tubing are: 0.183, 0.190, 0.180, 0.189, 0.190, 0.188, 0.186, 0.185.

    Find the 95% confidence interval for the population mean of inside diameter of the plastic tubing.

    a.  (0.183, 0.189)

    b.  (0.184, 0.188)

    c.  (0.181, 0.190)

    d.  None of the above

130. A quality audit is to be conducted within a particular company. The company has hired an independent contractor to conduct the audit. This is an example of:

    a.  an internal quality auditor.

    b.  an external quality auditor.

    c.  an auditee.

    d.  None of the above

131. The temperature of a chicken entrée prepared in a restaurant was collected in a performance improvement project. The team would like to compare the distribution of the data collected to the target temperature of 165 degrees Fahrenheit. Which of the following quality control tools is most appropriate to use?

    a.  Histogram

    b.  Scatter diagram

    c.  Pareto chart

    d.  Control chart

132. A double sampling plan is implemented with the following parameters: $n_1 = 75$, $c_1 = 2$, $r_1 = 5$, $n_2 = 75$, $c_2 = 4$, $r_2 = 7$. What is the probability that a decision is made (accept or reject the lot) on the first sample if the percent nonconforming $p = 0.015$?

    a.  0.4092

    b.  0.2697

    c.  0.3211

    d.  0.5908

133. The mean time to failure for a model of dishwasher is 115 months. What is the probability of a given dishwasher failing by 115 months of operation? Assume the reliability of the dishwasher has an exponential distribution.

    a.  0.368

    b.  2.718

    c.  0.009

    d.  0.632

134. A study on a random sample of 16 cars was done to evaluate the relationship of age of the car and its cost. The ANOVA table below displays the results of a regression analysis. At the 5% significance level, what conclusions can be drawn from these results?

| Source | df | SS | MS | F | p-value |
|---|---|---|---|---|---|
| Regression | 1 | 429.68 | 429.68 | 52.53 | 0.000 |
| Error | | 14 | 114.55 | 8.18 | |
| Total | | 15 | 544.23 | | |

   a. The age of the car does not have a significant effect on the cost.

   b. The intercept of the regression equation, $\beta_0$, is equal to 0.

   c. The age of the car has a significant effect on the cost.

   d. The intercept of the regression equation, $\beta_0$, does not equal 0.

135. A team at a factory is monitoring the average number of defects in TV screens. Twenty-eight TV screens are randomly selected each day over a 50-day period. The average number of defects per TV screen was found to be $\bar{u} = 0.214$. What is the lower control limit for a corresponding $u$-chart?

   a. 0.476

   b. 0

   c. 0.018

   d. 0.410

136. A benefit of implementing an FMEA is that it:

   a. is inexpensive.

   b. must be used with other quality programs such as Six Sigma.

   c. helps a team identify and eliminate the negative effects of potential failures before they occur.

   d. All of the above

137. In a lean system, what is another name for waste?

   a. Kanban

   b. Kaizen

c. Seiton

d. Muda

138. 100% inspection is most appropriate when:

   a. the cost of inspection is high.

   b. destructive sampling is required.

   c. the fraction of nonconforming products is high.

   d. inspection of products causes inspector fatigue.

139. What probability distribution is required for the results of a capability study to be considered valid?

   a. Normal

   b. Binomial

   c. Poisson

   d. Exponential

140. A team decided to change the range of temperature from 150–250 °F to 175–225 °F in an experimental design. What is a potential disadvantage of changing the range of this factor?

   a. Increasing the experimental error

   b. Missing an important effect

   c. Increasing the cost of the experiment

   d. Increasing the measurement error

141. Consider the histogram below. What shape does this distribution have?

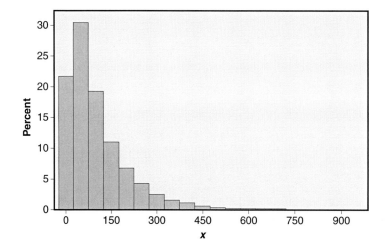

a. Symmetric

b. Right-skewed

c. Left-skewed

d. Bimodal

142. As the degrees of freedom go to infinity, what distribution does Student's *t*-distribution become?

a. Chi-square

b. Uniform

c. Standard normal

d. *F*

143. Design inputs are requirements for products and processes. These inputs are often related to:

a. regulatory requirements.

b. customer needs.

c. product capabilities.

d. All of the above

144. Employees at a pharmacy continuously look for ways to make their jobs easier. They color-coded cabinets to better identify materials. They placed check sheets near supplies to keep track of when they needed to be replaced. Finally, they created a document for employees to use when they called customers, in order to avoid rework. Which of the following improvement methods have these employees been using?

a. Six Sigma

b. Kaizen

c. Reengineering

d. TQM

145. When compared with attributes sampling plans, variables sampling plans:

a. provide information on how well a process is operating.

b. are generally less expensive to implement.

c. are able to monitor multiple quality characteristics at once.

d. are easier to administer in practice.

146. Two methods for filling a bottle are being compared at a factory. The two methods have known standard deviations $\sigma_1 = 0.05$ oz and $\sigma_2 = 0.04$ oz, respectively. A random sample of $n_1 = 24$ bottles using method 1 and an independent random sample of $n_2 = 25$ bottles using method 2 are collected. The mean volume using method 1 is 15.95 oz, and the mean volume using method 2 is 16.02 oz. Test the hypothesis that the two methods have different mean volumes (use $\alpha = 0.10$). What is your conclusion?

    a. Reject $H_0$, conclude that the two means are the same.

    b. Reject $H_0$, conclude that the two means are not the same.

    c. Do not reject $H_0$, conclude that the two means are the same.

    d. Do not reject $H_0$, conclude that the two means are not the same.

147. Which of the following lean tools for helping to reduce changeover times has been attributed to Shigeo Shingo and the Toyota Production System?

    a. Cycle time

    b. Takt time

    c. Standardized work

    d. SMED

148. In a test of a component of a machine, 350 components were tested for eight hours and 62 components failed. If the mean time to repair these components is three hours, what is the steady-state availability of this component?

    a. 0.9378

    b. 0.0622

    c. 45.25

    d. 0.0221

149. Which of the following characteristics of a company's customers is considered continuous data?

    a. Age

    b. Gender

    c. Number of members in the household

    d. Hair color

150. Which of the following graphical methods will assess the assumption of normality in the analysis of a designed experiment?

    a.  Normal probability plot of residuals

    b.  Scatter plot of residuals versus predicted values

    c.  Scatter plot of predicted versus actual values

    d.  Run chart

151. Which of the following statements is true regarding the second region of the bathtub curve?

    a.  The failure rate is increasing.

    b.  The failure rate is decreasing.

    c.  The uniform distribution is a good model for the reliability in this region.

    d.  None of the above

152. Suppose the number of errors in an invoice at a company has the probability mass function (written in table form) shown below. What is the variance of the number of errors?

| Number of errors X | 0 | 1 | 2 | 3 | 4 |
|---|---|---|---|---|---|
| Probability | 0.86 | 0.06 | 0.04 | 0.03 | 0.01 |

    a.  0.27

    b.  0.5771

    c.  0.7597

    d.  0

153. Which of the following criteria must a condition have to be qualified as a problem?

    a.  Variable performance from a set standard.

    b.  Deviation from perception.

    c.  The cause of the problem is unknown.

    d.  All of the above

154. In a resolution IV fractional factorial experiment, two-factor interactions are confounded with:

    a. main effects.

    b. three-factor or higher interactions.

    c. two-factor or higher interactions.

    d. no other effects.

155. A team is doing a project on errors in customers' files. What type of sampling is appropriate for this project?

    a. Double sampling

    b. Sequential sampling

    c. Stratified sampling

    d. Simple random sampling

156. Which of the following is not an assumption required for use and interpretation in regression analysis?

    a. The errors $e_i$ are normally distributed with mean zero.

    b. The errors $e_i$ are dependent.

    c. The errors $e_i$ are independent.

    d. The errors $e_i$ have constant variance.

157. A sample of size 24 is drawn from a population that follows a normal distribution with mean 97 and variance 85. What is the standard error of the sample mean?

    a. 1.88

    b. 3.54

    c. 97

    d. 17.35

158. A hospital denotes different areas by color (for example, blue, pink, green). In each area, room signs and floors are painted with their designated color. This is an example of:

    a. visual control.

   b.  standardized work.

   c.  kanban.

   d.  waste.

159. The distribution on which $c$-charts are based is called:

   a.  Poisson.

   b.  binomial.

   c.  hypergeometric.

   d.  normal.

160. A dimension of a component has specifications of $10.80 \pm 2.50$. The process data are normally distributed with mean 10.45 and standard deviation 1.05. What fraction of components will have this dimension within the specification limits?

   a.  0.9966

   b.  0.0034

   c.  0.0236

   d.  0.9764

161. Which of the following is a property of Dodge-Romig sampling tables?

   a.  They do not require an estimate of the process average nonconforming.

   b.  They are advantageous when the process quality worsens.

   c.  They use the actual measurements of sample products to make decisions on quality.

   d.  They minimize average total inspection.

162. In one year, a company spent more than $500,000 on warranty issues. This cost would be categorized as:

   a.  prevention cost.

   b.  appraisal cost.

   c.  internal failure cost.

   d.  external failure cost.

163. A two-way ANOVA hypothesis test was used to test the effects of two factors on a response variable $y$. What conclusions can be drawn from the ANOVA table below?

| Source | df | SS | MS | F | p-value |
|--------|----|----|----|----|---------|
| A | 2 | 1918.50 | 959.250 | 9.25 | 0.015 |
| B | 1 | 21.33 | 21.333 | 0.21 | 0.666 |
| AB | 2 | 561.17 | 280.583 | 2.71 | 0.145 |
| Error | 6 | 622.00 | 103.667 | | |
| Total | 11 | 3123.00 | | | |

   a. There is a significant interaction effect between factors A and B.

   b. Factor B has a significant effect on the response $y$.

   c. Factor A has a significant effect on the response $y$.

   d. Both factors A and B have a significant effect on the response $y$.

164. A supplier has received an order from one of their customers. They must complete an order of 750 items in a daytime shift that is 10 hours long. The cycle time for this process is 40 seconds. Without changing their current production methods, will the supplier be able to meet the customer's demands?

   a. No, since cycle time ≤ takt time.

   b. Yes, since cycle time ≤ takt time.

   c. No, since cycle time > takt time.

   d. Yes, since cycle time > takt time.

165. Consider an experiment with seven factors each at two levels. The complete defining relation is $I$ = ABCDF = ABDEG = CEFG. What resolution is this design?

   a. Resolution III

   b. Resolution IV

   c. Resolution V

   d. Full-factorial design

166. Paired data collected from a process are: (5.2, 26.7), (6.1, 27.5), (3.2, 24.9), (4.6, 25.5). What is the correlation coefficient for these data?

    a. 0.92

    b. 0.96

    c. 21.74

    d. –0.96

167. Common development stages teams often progress through are known as *forming, storming, norming,* and *performing.* In the "forming" stage:

    a. individuals begin to shift from personal concerns to needs of the team.

    b. the team's mission is clarified and specific roles are identified.

    c. team members still think and act as individuals instead of impacting as a team.

    d. team has matured and is working in the best interest of the team and team goals.

168. What fraction of all rechargeable batteries fail by 10 hours if the MTBF is eight hours? Assume the reliability of these batteries has an exponential distribution.

    a. 12.50%

    b. 28.65%

    c. 71.35%

    d. 87.50%

169. The graph below shows the salaries of employees at a company. What measure of central tendency would be most appropriate to describe these data?

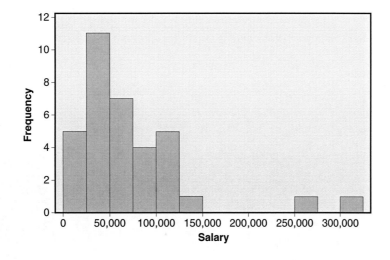

a.  Mode

b.  Mean

c.  Median

d.  Standard deviation

170. What is the primary purpose of a process decision program chart?

a.  To visualize the relationship between two sets of factors

b.  To assess a process implementation plan during the initial phases of operations

c.  To manage the schedule of a complex process

d.  To evaluate differing options based on a set of criteria

171. A hospital is trying to improve patient flow in their emergency department by tracking patients. Which of the following would help most in this endeavor?

a.  Control charts

b.  Radio frequency identification

c.  OC curves

d.  Affinity diagram

172. Which of the following is one of Deming's 14 points?

a.  Institute barriers that stand between the hourly worker and his right to pride of workmanship.

b.  Institute modern methods of training on the job.

c.  15% of quality problems are due to the system.

d.  85% of quality problems are due to management.

173. Which of the following statements about rational subgroups is *not* correct?

a.  Within-sample variation is minimized.

b.  Between-sample variation is maximized.

c.  Rational subgrouping is not important when constructing control charts.

d.  With rational subgroups, there is a greater probability of variation between successive samples.

174. Gale and Wood (1994) introduced seven tools of customer value analysis. They described different perspectives on what customers believe is of value in a product or service. Which of the following would often be considered a *value* by the customer?

    a. Quality

    b. Inconsistent service

    c. Lack of durability

    d. Difficult to access

175. Consider the following results of a $2^3$ full-factorial design with two replicates. Assuming the normality and variance assumptions are valid, which terms have a significant effect on the response variable?

| Source | df | SS | MS | F | p-value |
|---|---|---|---|---|---|
| A | 1 | 16.0 | 16.0 | 3.20 | 0.1114 |
| B | 1 | 12.0 | 12.0 | 2.40 | 0.1599 |
| C | 1 | 5.0 | 5.0 | 1.00 | 0.3466 |
| AB | 1 | 2.5 | 2.5 | 0.50 | 0.4996 |
| AC | 1 | 1.5 | 1.5 | 0.30 | 0.5988 |
| BC | 1 | 0.5 | 0.5 | 0.10 | 0.7599 |
| ABC | 1 | 0.25 | 0.25 | 0.05 | 0.8287 |
| Error | 8 | 40.0 | 5.0 | | |
| Total | 15 | | | | |

    a. A and B

    b. All main effects and two-factor interactions

    c. A and B only

    d. None of the main effects or interactions

176. A bottling factory claims that the volume of soda filled in bottles is 18 oz. You want to test whether the true mean volume of soda is different than 18 oz. The volume of a random sample of 24 bottles had a mean of 17.98 oz with a standard deviation of 0.03 oz. Using a significance level of 5%, what is the critical value for this hypothesis test?

   a.  ±2.069

   b.  2.069

   c.  −3.266

   d.  ±1.96

177. A tool is designed so that, upon assembly, a component can be attached to the tool in only one position. What type of prevention action does this describe?

   a.  Fail-safe device

   b.  Redundancy

   c.  Magnification of senses

   d.  Special control device

178. The length of five components was measured by two inspectors (data shown below). Assuming the data follow a normal distribution, find a 95% confidence interval for the difference in the mean length measured by the two inspectors.

| Component | 1 | 2 | 3 | 4 | 5 |
|---|---|---|---|---|---|
| Inspector A | 10.2 | 9.8 | 10.1 | 10.3 | 10.4 |
| Inspector B | 10.0 | 9.9 | 10.3 | 10.0 | 10.3 |

   a.  (−0.367, 0.487)

   b.  (−0.254, 0.374)

   c.  (−0.404, 0.524)

   d.  (−0.197, 0.317)

179. The time between arrivals at a store has an exponential distribution with mean four minutes. What is the probability that the time between arrivals is more than five minutes?

   a.  0

b. 0.2865

c. 0.7135

d. 3.4903

180. Consider the ANOVA table below for a one-factor experiment with a blocking variable. How many levels are there of factor A and the blocking factor?

| Source of variation | df | SS | MS | F |
|---|---|---|---|---|
| Factor A | 5 | 198.0 | 49.5 | 12.05 |
| Block | 4 | 101.75 | 33.92 | |
| Error | 20 | 79.25 | 6.60 | |
| Total | 29 | 379.00 | | |

a. 5, 4

b. 6, 5

c. 4, 5

d. 20, 29

181. A group of operators in a semiconductor factory have an idea to improve their work flow. However, upper management has been reluctant to explore this idea. How might this group of operators classify this response?

a. Waiting

b. Excess motion

c. Defect correction

d. Lost creativity

182. Calculate the sample variance of the following observations: 5.3, 8.6, 7.2, 9.1, 7.5, 3.5.

a. 4.459

b. 3.716

c. 2.112

d. 1.928

183. The wait times of 30 consecutive patients at a clinic were recorded. The team determined that $\bar{X}$ = 17.90 and $\overline{MR}$ = 1.75. What are the upper and lower control limits for the moving range chart?

    a. UCL = 5.72, LCL = 0

    b. UCL = 22.55, LCL = 13.25

    c. UCL = 4.65, LCL = 0

    d. UCL = 3.29, LCL = 0

184. A team has collected measurement data from a machine at a factory. To determine whether the data are autocorrelated, which of the following methods could the team use?

    a. Trend analysis

    b. Goodness-of-fit test

    c. Chi-square test

    d. Designed experiment

185. Which of the following events is *not* a source of special cause variation?

    a. Dull tools

    b. Large change in raw materials

    c. Slight variation in ambient humidity

    d. Broken machine

186. Consider the following $\bar{X}$ chart from a normally distributed process. What conclusions can be drawn from this control chart?

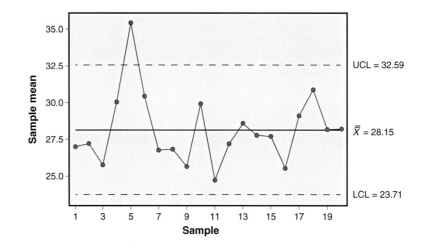

a. The process is out of control.

b. The process is stable.

c. The process is operating within the specifications.

d. The process is operating outside the specifications.

187. Maintaining risk at or below an acceptable level is part of:

a. risk control.

b. risk overisght.

c. risk management planning.

d. None of the above

188. The test statistic for a hypothesis test for two population variances follows which distribution under the null hypothesis?

a. Normal

b. Binomial

c. $\chi^2$

d. $F$

189. Which of the following improvement methodologies provides a framework to iteratively improve a process?

a. PDCA

b. TQM

c. Reengineering

d. TOC

190. A stable, normally distributed process has specifications $15.50 \pm 1.25$. A sample of data from the process had a mean $\mu = 16.50$ and standard deviation $\sigma_1 = 0.10$. Is the process considered capable?

a. Yes, since $C_p = 25$

b. Yes, since $C_{pk} = 7.5$

c. No, since $C_p = 25$

d. No, since $C_{pk} = 0.83$

191. A company has spare parts that need to be evaluated. This would be an example of:

    a. prevention costs.

    b. appraisal costs.

    c. internal failure costs.

    d. external failure costs.

192. Consider the following system where the reliability of each component is displayed within each box. What is the reliability of the overall system?

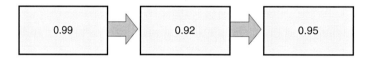

    a. 0.8653

    b. 0.9999

    c. 0.95

    d. None of the above

193. Consider the control frame below.

| ⟋⟋ | Ⓛ | 0.01 | A | B | C |

    "B" represents:

    a. primary datum.

    b. secondary datum.

    c. tertiary datum.

    d. modifier.

194. True/False. A corrective maintenance policy is an efficient way to handle repairs of a system.

    a. True

    b. False

195. An online store is reviewing causes for its large number of customer returns. A Pareto chart revealed that the most frequent reason for returns cited by customers was "Item not what I ordered." How would the store classify this type of waste?

    a. Overproduction

    b. Defect correction

    c. Excess movement of materials

    d. Excess processing

196. A machine has six subsystems and will fail when four or more of these subsystems fail. What type of system design does this machine have?

    a. Series system

    b. Parallel system

    c. *k*-out-of-*n* system

    d. Mixed parallel

197. An experiment has eight factors at two levels each. The experiment has 64 runs. What is the experimental design called?

    a. Full-factorial design

    b. Half-fractional factorial design

    c. Taguchi design

    d. None of the above

198. *Criticality* measures:

    a. the likelihood of a failure occurring.

    b. the consequences of a failure mode and its frequency of occurrence.

    c. the likelihood of detecting a failure once it has occurred.

    d. the severity of a failure if it occurs.

199. True/False. According to Shingo, it is ideal to move as many activities from external to internal as possible in order to reduce changeover times.

    a. True

    b. False

200. The standard deviation of a Poisson distribution is 3.04. What is the mean of this distribution?

    a. Not enough information provided

    b. 1.74

    c. 20.91

    d. 9.24

201. The need for an international standard like ISO 9000 arose:

    a. because national standards are incomplete.

    b. to provide consistency in terms, vocabulary, and requirements.

    c. because industry-specific standards were simply carbon copies of national standards.

    d. None of the above

202. The Malcolm Baldrige National Quality Award emphasizes:

    a. results.

    b. requirements.

    c. procedures.

    d. None of the above

203. Last month, a local company reported the following quality costs.

| Incoming inspection | $ 60,000 |
|---|---|
| Design support | $ 12,000 |
| Field trials | $110,000 |

    What is the total prevention cost for last month?

    a. $12,000

    b. $122,000

    c. $100,000

    d. $77,000

204. A fault tree analysis (FTA) is a useful tool for prioritizing risks. One of the drawbacks or limitations of the FTA is:

    a.  it can not be used to identify combinations of failure modes, only single failure modes.

    b.  it only uses binary data such as failure/no failure.

    c.  it is too complicated since it does not require the user to know anything about the process or product.

    d.  None of the above

205. A risk priority number is an output from a(n):

    a.  flowchart.

    b.  QFD.

    c.  FMEA.

    d.  expert opinion.

## SOLUTIONS

1. a; Pre-control charts do not provide information on how variability can be reduced or how to bring a process into control. They should only be used for processes with a capability ratio greater than one. Poor capability in a pre-control chart will indicate that assignable causes are present when in fact there are no assignable causes of variation. Small sample sizes in a pre-control chart will reduce the chart's ability to detect moderate to large shifts. Pre-control charts are useful in initial setup operations to determine whether a process is centered between the tolerances. [VI.F.7]

2. b;

$$\sigma^2_{\text{Measurement error}} = \sigma^2_{\text{Reproducibility}} + \sigma^2_{\text{Repeatability}};$$

therefore,

$$\sigma^2_{\text{Measurement error}} = \sqrt{\sigma^2_{\text{Reproducibility}} + \sigma^2_{\text{Repeatability}}} = \sqrt{0.9214^2 + 0.5873^2} = 1.0927.$$

Recall that standard deviation is not additive; variance is. [IV.F]

3. b; *Attribute data* is the term used to describe discrete data in quality control. Wait time, processing costs, and thickness can each be measured on a continuous scale. The number of filing errors can only take on a countable set of numbers, and is considered discrete, or attribute, data. [VI.A.1]

4. a; A series system is made up of $n$ components connected end-to-end. Therefore, if one component fails, the entire system fails. [III.E.2]

5. b; Lean deals with eliminating waste. Lean Six Sigma focuses on eliminating waste and minimizing variability. [I.A.1]

6. d; The central limit theorem states that if the sample size $n$ is sufficiently large, then the sample mean $\bar{X}$ follows approximately a normal distribution with mean $\mu_{\bar{X}} = \mu$ and standard deviation $\sigma_{\bar{X}} = \sigma / \sqrt{n}$.

   In this case, $\mu = 24$, $\sigma = 5.5$, and $n = 32$. Therefore,

   $$\sigma_{\bar{X}} = 5.5 / \sqrt{32}.$$

   [VI.C.2]

7. b; The goal is to identify limits and action levels that will result in a process or product that meets all of its requirements. [III.D]

8. a; The only appraisal cost is incoming inspection. [II.E]

9. c; Control plans include detailed reaction plans that should be followed when the control method detects a problem in the process. The reaction plan details the steps the operator should take when the process has a problem. [IV.A]

10. d; The summary statistics for the sample are

   $$\bar{x} = \frac{20 + 29 + 40 + 25}{4} = 28.50; \ R = 40 - 20 = 20.$$

   From the information given,

   $$\bar{x} = 26.75, \ \bar{R} = 8.10, \ n = 4$$

   The control limits for the $\bar{X}$ chart are:

   $$\text{UCL} = \bar{\bar{x}} + A_2\bar{R} = 26.75 + 0.729(8.10) = 32.65$$

   $$\text{LCL} = \bar{\bar{x}} - A_2\bar{R} = 24.8 - 0.729(8.10) = 20.85$$

The control limits for the R chart are:

$$UCL = D_4\bar{R} = (2.282)(8.10) = 18.48$$

$$LCL = D_3\bar{R} = (0)(5.50) = 0$$

$A_2$, $D_3$, and $D_4$ can be found in Appendix C of *The Certified Quality Engineer Handbook*, Third Edition for $n = 4$.

Since $\bar{X} = 28.50$ is within the LCL and UCL for the $\bar{X}$ chart, and $R = 20$ is greater than the UCL for the $R$-chart, only the range was outside the control limits. [VI.F.5]

11. b; The third region of a bathtub curve is the wear-out region, where there is an increasing failure rate over time. Components that rotate or have alternating motions frequently wear out over time. [III.E.3]

12. c; All performance measures should be achievable and aligned with strategic goals. In addition, the focus should be on the "vital few." One should avoid using too many measures or metrics. [I.B.2.c]

13. d; Interrelationship digraphs provide a means to identify sequential or cause-and-effect relationships of a problem or situation. Affinity diagrams are used to organize general thoughts and ideas about a topic. Tree diagrams are used to visualize hierarchical events of a process, and process decision program charts (PDPCs) help to evaluate a process implementation plan at a high level. [V.B]

14. b; When a product defect is discovered, the material review board (MRB) determines what corrective actions to take. [IV.B.4]

15. c; $\alpha = 0.10$ and $p$-value = 0.23. Using the $p$-value approach to hypothesis testing, if the $p$-value < $\alpha$, we will reject $H_0$. If $p$-value > $\alpha$, we do not reject $H_0$. Since 0.23 > 0.10, we do not reject $H_0$ and conclude that the two means are the same. [VI.D.2]

16. d; The risk priority number (RPN) is determined by multiplying the three components of risk together: severity, occurrence, and detection. Each of these components is given a score on a 1 to 10 scale. Therefore, the maximum possible value of RPN is $10 \times 10 \times 10 = 1000$. [III.E.4]

17. c; Process improvement teams should also be cross-functional, consisting of people from many different departments/areas within the company (and possibly externally, such as customers and suppliers). [I.D.4]

18. a; A part passes inspection with a go/no-go gage if the part mates with the "go" end and does not mate with the "no-go" end. Since this part mated with both ends, it did not pass the no-go inspection. Therefore, the part should be rejected. [IV.D.1]

19. c; Using a QFD to identify the needs of a training program can provide a more focused approach to design and delivery of the program. [II.F.15]

20. c; In the problem identification phase, the team identifies sources for improvement and develops a clear problem statement. In the correction phase, the team develops feasible solutions to the problem and recommends the best choice to implement. In the recurrence control phase, the team standardizes the solution to ensure that the problem does not reoccur and prevent backsliding. Finally, in the effectiveness assessment phase, the team continues monitoring the process to identify additional opportunities for improvement. [V.E]

21. b; In a Weibull probability plot, the data are plotted against a percentile based on the Weibull distribution. Since the points in this probability plot fall in a straight line, the Weibull distribution is a reasonable model for the time to failure. [VI.A.7]

22. d; In this problem, a "success" is a patient fall. Therefore, $x = 6$ and $n = 56$. The sample proportion is then

$$\hat{p} = \frac{5}{56} = 0.1071. \ \alpha = 0.10, \ Z_{\alpha/2} = Z_{0.05} = 1.645.$$

The corresponding 90% confidence interval is

$$\hat{p} - z_{\alpha/2}\sqrt{\frac{\hat{p}(1-\hat{p})}{n}} \leq p \leq \hat{p} + z_{\alpha/2}\sqrt{\frac{\hat{p}(1-\hat{p})}{n}}$$

$$0.1071 - 1.645\sqrt{\frac{0.1071(1-0.1071)}{56}} \leq p \leq 0.1071 + 1.645\sqrt{\frac{0.1071(1-0.1071)}{56}}$$

$$0.0391 \leq p \leq 0.1751.$$

We are 90% confident that the true proportion of patient falls in the hospital is between 3.91% and 17.51%. [VI.D.1]

23. d; The $\bar{X}$ control chart reflects within-sample variability, which is related to gage repeatability. If the gage is capable, then it should be able to distinguish between parts. Therefore, we would expect many of the points to plot outside the control limits. In this case, most of the points are within the control limits; this indicates that the gage can not distinguish between parts. [IV.F]

24. a; In the prototype phase, a working model is created and tested. One goal is to determine whether the product/process will perform as intended. [III.B.1]

25. a; From the properties of the cumulative distribution function, P(a < Z < b) = P(Z < b) – P(Z < a). Therefore, using a standard normal table,

$$P(-1.02 < Z < 0.58) = P(Z < 0.58) - P(Z < -1.02) = 0.7190 - 0.1539 = 0.5651.$$

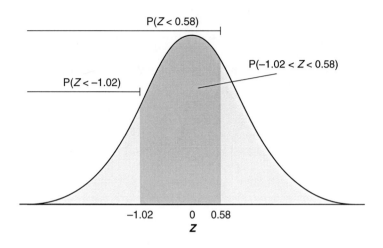

[VI.C.1]

26. d; Given the lot size is 100, the sample size code letter from the ANSI/ASQ Z1.4-2003 (R2013) sampling tables for normal, level II sampling is F. Regardless of the AQL level, the required sample size is then $n = 20$ (Table II-A). [IV.C.2]

27. c; The reliability function at time $t$ is defined as the probability that a randomly selected unit will survive for a time greater than time $t$. The cumulative distribution function of failure $F(t)$ is the probability that a randomly selected unit fails by time $t$. Since $F(t) + R(t) = 1$, $F(t) = 1 - (998/1000) = 2/1000$. [III.E.1]

28. b; Genichi Taguchi proposed signal-to-noise ratios in order to optimize the response variable $y$ and minimize the standard deviation.

    If the goal is to maximize the response variable $y$, the S/N ratio is calculated as

    $$S/N = \bar{y}/S.$$

    If the goal of the experiment is to minimize $y$, the S/N ratio may be calculated as

    $$S/N = \frac{1}{\bar{y}S}.$$

    If the goal of the experiment is to make $y$ as close to a target value $N$ as possible, the S/N ratio is calculated as

    $$S/N = \frac{1}{|\bar{y} - N|S}.$$

[VI.H.6]

29. c; A date is on an interval scale. There are meaningful differences between two dates, but there is no absolute zero. Dates can be added or subtracted. For example, you can calculate the number of days between two dates by subtracting them. However, you can not meaningfully multiply or divide two dates. [VI.A.2]

30. d; Standardized work means that each activity is done the same way every time. Because each employee performs the activities the same way, having standardized work in practice will help reduce process variation and provide more consistent (and likely better) products. Standardized work can also help simplify activities downstream. [V.D]

31. b; Given: $n = 35$ and Accept line $= 0.1043n - 1.2486$. The acceptance number can be found by plugging $n = 35$ into the accept line equation:

$$\text{Accept line} = (0.1043)(35) - 1.2486 = 2.4019.$$

The acceptance values are rounded down to the nearest integer to get the acceptance number. Therefore, the acceptance number is 2. [IV.C.2]

32. d; Undercontrol, also called *underadjustment*, occurs when a process operator fails to respond to the presence of special cause variation. *Undercontrol* occurs when a control chart has indicated out-of-control behavior, but the process operator does not adjust the process. [VI.F.2]

33. a; An app that occasionally crashes during use would not cause an injury or result in a large economic loss. Therefore, this would be classified as a minor defect. [IV.B.3]

34. a; This notation indicates that there are five independent variables (factors) and each factor is run at three levels. There are a total of $3^5 = 243$ treatment combinations in this experiment. This notation does not give any information on the number of responses or replicates. [VI.H.1]

35. b; The dashed OC curve is better for the manufacturer. The probability of accepting the lot is still very high for large values of percentage nonconforming. The other OC curve would be better suited for the company. [IV.C.1]

36. b; The failure function $F(t)$ is the probability that a randomly selected unit drawn from a population fails by time $t$:

$$F(t) = 1 - R(t) = 1 - e^{-\lambda t}.$$

Since

$$\lambda = 0.0008, \ \text{MTTF} = \frac{1}{\lambda} = \frac{1}{0.0008} = 1250.$$

Therefore,

$$F(\text{MTTF}) = F(1250) = 1 - R(1250) = 1 - e^{-0.0008(1250)} = 1 - 0.3679 = 0.6321.$$

[III.E.2]

37. c; The box plot for store A is much tighter than that for store B. This indicates that there is more variability in wait time at store B compared to store A. Note that the distribution of wait times at both stores is approximately symmetric. [VI.A.6]

38. c; An interaction plot can show differences in the mean response for the different levels of factors A and B. This interaction plot indicates that there is a significant interaction between factors A and B. Changing from level 1 to level 2 of factor A, the response is quite different for the low level of factor B. [VI.D.5]

39. c; The supplier's physical location may be of interest to the company but is not necessarily a part of the rating process. It may or may not be included as it is written here. Evaluating or rating on ethnicity would not only be an unethical practice, it is also an illegal one. [I.H.8]

40. c; DMAIC is made up of five phases used in an improvement process: define, measure, analyze, improve, and control. In the analyze phase, the team has already clearly defined the problem and related metrics, and have measured the performance of the process. The team now investigates the root cause of variation in the process or poor performance. [V.C]

41. a; Using the Poisson approximation for the binomial distribution, the probability of acceptance is

$$P_a = P(d \le c) = \Sigma_{d=0}^{c} \frac{(np)^d e^{-np}}{d!} = \Sigma_{d=0}^{2} \frac{(80 \times 0.025)^d e^{-80 \times 0.025}}{d!} = 0.677.$$

Note that $np = 80 \times 0.025 = 2$ is the mean of the binomial distribution, and is therefore the parameter for the Poisson distribution. [IV.C.1]

42. b; This is a hypothesis test for a single population mean $\mu$ where the population variance is known. The hypotheses for this test are $H_0 : \mu = 120$ versus $H_a : \mu > 120$. The test statistic is:

$$z_0 = \frac{\bar{x} - \mu_0}{\sigma / \sqrt{n}} = \frac{124 - 120}{1.25 / \sqrt{15}} = 12.39$$

Note that we reject $H_0$ if $z_0 > z_\alpha = z_{0.05} = 1.645$. Since $12.39 > 1.645$, we reject $H_0$ and conclude that the mean tensile strength is more than 120 psi. [VI.D.2]

43. a; One interpretation of the failure function $F(t)$ is the fraction of all units in the population that fail by time $t$. Since

$$\text{MTTF} = 525, \ \lambda = \frac{1}{\text{MTTF}} = 1/525.$$

Therefore,

$$F(1000) = 1 - R(1000) = 1 - e^{-\lambda(1000)} = 1 - e^{-\frac{1000}{525}} = 1 - 0.1489 = 0.8511.$$

Approximately 85% of the population will fail by 1000 hours. [III.E.2]

44. d; The precision of a measurement system consists of *repeatability* and *reproducibility*. Gage bias, linearity, and stability describe the *accuracy* of a measurement system. [IV.F]

45. c; Before calculating the statistics associated with the variables or fitting a regression model, the team should first plot the data in a scatter diagram. The scatter diagram will indicate whether there is a relationship between the two variables. If there is a *linear* relationship, then the team may wish to calculate the correlation coefficient. Comparing the histograms individually will not provide information on how the value of one variable changes with the other variable. [V.A]

46. a; Since A and B are statistically independent,

$$P(A \cap B) = P(A)P(B) = (0.62)(0.09) = 0.0558.$$

[VI.B.3]

47. c; *Lean* deals with eliminating waste. Lean Six Sigma focuses on eliminating waste and minimizing variability. [I.A.1]

48. d; In the problem identification phase, the team identifies sources for improvement and develops a clear problem statement. In the correction phase, the team develops feasible solutions to the problem and recommends the best choice to implement. In the recurrence control phase, the team standardizes the solution to ensure that the problem does not reoccur. Finally, in the effectiveness assessment phase, the team continues monitoring the process to identify additional opportunities for improvement. [V.E]

49. c; Measurement assurance includes information on the contribution of error by technicians or a laboratory's procedures. Calibration is typically the focus when testing an instrument, and little consideration is given to errors made by operators or the environment in which it's used. [IV.E]

50. a; When the control in place is not adequate for the risk, or no control has been put in place for a significant risk, it is called a *gap* or *control gap*. [VII.C.1]

51. b; There are two factors of interest in the experiment. However, there is also a possibility that the day the experiment is performed could have an effect on the response variable. There is no interest in whether or not there are significant differences between levels of day. Therefore, day is a blocking factor, and a randomized block design is appropriate. [VI.H.5]

52. b; *Readability* is defined as the ease of reading the instrument scale while measuring some component. The readability of the equipment, however, will not necessarily result in more accurate results in measurement. [IV.E]

53. d; The control chart indicated there was an out-of-control point. This means that the process is not stable; there is special cause variation present in the system. Therefore, the capability of the process is unknown. [VI.G.2, VI.G.3]

54. d; The sample correlation coefficient measures the strength of the linear relationship between two variables. The scatter plot shows that as $x$ increases, $y$ decreases. This indicates that there is a negative correlation. The correlation coefficient only takes values between –1 and +1. The closer the value is to –1 or +1, the stronger the linear relationship, so there is a strong negative correlation between these two variables. [VI.E.2]

55. d; Typical calibration control systems include the following procedures: evaluation of equipment to determine its capability, identification of calibration requirements, selection of standards to perform calibration, selection of the methods to carry out the measurements for the calibration, and more. [IV.E]

56. a; The hazard function is defined as

$$h(t) = \frac{f(t)}{R(t)} = \frac{\text{\# of failures per unit time}}{\text{\# components tested per unit time}}.$$

Therefore, one interpretation of the hazard function is an instantaneous rate of failure at a given time $t$. [III.E.1]

57. b; As stated in the problem, the estimate should be within 0.05 MPa of the true average. This means we will allow the estimate to be at most 0.05 MPa less than the average or at most 0.05 MPa greater than the true average. The margin of error is E = 0.05. Furthermore,

$$\sigma = 0.50, \ \alpha = 0.01, \ Z_{\alpha/2} = Z_{0.005} = 2.576.$$

The minimum sample size needed is:

$$n \geq \left(\frac{\sigma Z_{\alpha/2}}{E}\right)^2 = \left(\frac{0.50(2.576)}{0.05}\right)^2 = 663.58.$$

Therefore, the minimum sample size of cement would be $n = 664$. [VI.D.1]

58. d; The risk associated with each potential failure mode is assigned a risk priority number (RPN). The RPN is made up of three components: severity, occurrence, and detection. [III.E.4]

59. c; Plug gages are typically used to assess conformance of inside dimensions of a part. Ring and snap gages are used to assess outside dimensions. Splines are typically used to check special features. Micrometers are used for linear measurements. [IV.D.1]

60. b; From the information provided, $\bar{p} = 0.045$, $m = 15$, $n = 150$.

The new sample number nonconforming is $x = 18$.

The control limits for the *np* chart are:

$$\text{UCL} = n\bar{p} + 3\sqrt{n\bar{p}(1-\bar{p})} = 150(0.045) + 3\sqrt{150(0.045)(1-0.045)} = 14.36$$

$$\text{LCL} = n\bar{p} - 3\sqrt{n\bar{p}(1-\bar{p})} = 150(0.045) - 3\sqrt{150(0.045)(1-0.045)} = 4.211$$

Since $x = 18$ lies above the UCL of the *np* chart, the sample is outside the control limits. [VI.F.5]

61. c; *Confounding* occurs when the effect of one factor is indistinguishable from the effect of another factor or factor interactions. An *interaction* is the change in response when two or more factors are interdependent. *Randomization* is the ordering of treatment combinations in a random sequence in order to reduce the effect of nuisance variables on the response. *Efficiency* in experimental design refers to an experiment that generates the maximum information while using a small number of runs and resources. [VI.H.3]

62. b; Type B OC curves are used to evaluate a sampling plan of a continuous process. These curves are constructed using either a binomial or Poisson distribution, depending on the scenario. Type A OC curves are used on a lot-by-lot basis for a product of a continuous process. [IV.C.1]

63. a; There is a sequence of eight points all increasing beginning with the 16th data point. One of the sensitizing rules to detect out-of-control behavior is six points in a row, all increasing or all decreasing. Note that a control chart does not provide information on whether the process is operating within the specification

limits. A process could be out of statistical control, but still operating within the specification limits. Similarly, a process could be in control, but not be within the specification limits. [VI.F.6]

64. d; The total variability is composed of the variability associated with the gage or measurement tool in addition to the part-to-part variability. Information on the part-to-part variability is not provided here, so there is not enough information to determine the total variability. Recall that

$$\sigma^2_{Total} = \sigma^2_{Gage} + \sigma^2_p = \sigma^2_{Reproducibility} + \sigma^2_{Repeatability} + \sigma^2_p,$$

where $\sigma^2_p$ denotes the part-to-part variability. [IV.F]

65. d; The lognormal, exponential, and chi-square distributions are all skewed to the right. They also can only assume positive values. [VI.C.1]

66. a; This is an example of waste due to inventory. The company has more inventory in storage than is necessary. As a result, they must pay to store these materials, which have no value to the customer. In addition, the company's high inventory also leads to additional losses when some of the products degrade before use. [V.D]

67. d; A reaction plan typically contains four elements: containment, diagnosis, verification, and disposition. The reaction plan should therefore include specific directions for the operators on how to dispose of material that was contained when a problem was detected in the process. Disposition may include scrap, rework, sort, use as-is, or return to vendor. [IV.A]

68. a; By plugging in the given value of Weight = 175 into the regression equation, we can predict the cholesterol. Cholesterol = 135 + 0.28 × (175) = 184. [VI.E.1]

69. a; In the *norming* phase, interpersonal conflicts have less impact on team dynamics and work. [I.D]

70. c; AOQ is the expected average quality of outgoing products. This value includes all accepted lots, plus all rejected lots that have been sorted 100%. [IV.C.1]

71. d; A material flow or traceability flowchart should include the critical components and their part numbers, a list of the vendors for each component, information on any internally manufactured part (including the date of manufacture), and detailed, computerized shipping records. [IV.B.1]

72. a; The machine has a $k$-out-of-$n$ system design where $k = 2$ and $n = 3$. The system reliability of a $k$-out-of-$n$ system is

$$R_s(t) = \sum_{i=k}^{n} \binom{n}{i} p^i (1-p)^{n-i},$$

where $p = 0.95$. Therefore, the system reliability is

$$R_s(t) = \binom{3}{2}(0.95)^2(0.05)^1 + \binom{3}{3}(0.95)^3(0.05)^0$$

$$= 3(0.95)^2(0.5)^1 + 1(0.95)^2(0.05)^1$$

$$= 0.1354 + 0.8574$$

$$= 0.9928.$$

[III.E.2]

73. c; Since there are no significant control-by-noise interactions, there is no robust design problem. The levels of the controllable factors are not significantly affected by changes in the noise variables. However, the controllable factors alone can still significantly affect the response. [VI.H.6]

74. a; Recall that

$$P_a = \Sigma_{d=0}^{c} \binom{n}{d} p^d (1-p)^{n-d}.$$

Therefore, as $c$ increases, the probability of acceptance will increase for a given fraction nonconforming and sample size. Consider, for example, an infinite lot size, a sample size $n = 15$, and fraction nonconforming $p = 0.10$. For acceptance numbers $c$, we have the following probability of acceptance:

| Acceptance number ($c$) | $P_a$ |
|---|---|
| 0 | 0.2059 |
| 1 | 0.5490 |
| 2 | 0.8159 |
| 3 | 0.9444 |

[IV.C.1]

75. b; The null and alternative hypotheses for this hypothesis test are

$$H_0 : \sigma^2 = 4 \text{ versus } H_a : \sigma^2 < 4.$$

The level of significance is $\alpha = 0.05$. This is a left-tailed test, so we would reject the null hypothesis if the test statistic is less than

$$\chi^2_{1-\alpha,k} = \chi^2_{0.95,21} = 11.591.$$

The test statistic is

$$\chi^2_0 = \frac{(n-1)s^2}{\sigma^2_0} = \frac{(22-1)1.75}{4} = 9.1875.$$

Since 9.1875 < 11.591, we reject the null hypothesis and conclude that the alternative hypothesis is true. At the 5% significance level, there is sufficient evidence to conclude that the variance of wait time is less than 4 minutes². [VI.D.2]

76. a; For a process operating at six sigma level quality, there are 3.4 defective parts per million. Not accounting for the 1.5σ shift from the mean, the process would have 0.002 defective parts per million. [V.C]

77. b; A full-factorial design is an experiment such that all treatment combinations of the factors are carried out. Therefore, the number of treatment combinations is 4 × 2 × 3 × 2 = 48. [VI.H.1]

78. b; Coordinate measuring machines are used for dimensional quality control for complex parts. They allow measurements to be completed within minutes. Precision spindles are used to make roundness measurements, micrometer calipers are used to take linear measurements, and go/no-go gages are used to assess specification conformance. [IV.D.1]

79. a; The failure rate, $\lambda$, is the number of failures divided by the total test time. Therefore,

$$\lambda = 28/(750 \times 5) = 0.0075.$$

The mean time to failure (MTTF) is $1/\lambda \approx 133$, assuming the life distribution is exponential. [III.E.2]

80. a; A type II error in hypothesis testing is the probability of failing to reject the null hypothesis when in fact the null hypothesis is false. This corresponds to the consumer's risk in acceptance sampling: the probability of accepting a lot that does not meet the LTPD level. [IV.C.1]

81. a; A pull system is emphasized in a lean enterprise. In a pull system, an action will initiate the next step in the process occurring. In this case, the customer's order initiates the completion of the computer. Using a pull system eases the burden of making accurate forecasts of customer demand and helps to reduce unused inventory. [V.D]

82. c; The test statistic for the test of independence follows a chi-square distribution with $(r-1)(c-1)$ degrees of freedom where $r$ represents the number of levels of the first factor and $c$ represents the number of levels of the second factor. We reject $H_0$ if

$$\chi_0^2 > \chi_{\alpha,(r-1)(c-1)}^2 = \chi_{0.10,2}^2 = 4.605.$$

Since

$$\chi_0^2 = 3.359 < 4.605,$$

we do not reject $H_0$, and conclude that the type of part produced (conforming or nonconforming) and time of day are independent. [VI.D.6]

83. b; The failure rate for this machine is $\lambda = 0.0008$ which means that the mean time between failures (MTBF) is

$$\frac{1}{\lambda} = \frac{1}{0.0008} = 1250 \text{ hours.}$$

Since MTTR = 48 hours, the steady-state availability of the machine is

$$A = \frac{\text{MTBF}}{\text{MTBF} + \text{MTTR}} = \frac{1250}{1250 + 48} = 0.9630.$$

[III.E.2]

84. c; While the illegible textbooks will not cause injury, they do represent a large economic loss as the company must replace all of the defective books. The company would classify this as a serious defect. [IV.B.3]

85. d; The central limit theorem states that the distribution of sample averages tends toward a normal distribution for large sample sizes. Because the population is highly skewed to the right, and the sample size is small ($n = 8$), the central limit theorem does not apply here. Samples size of greater than 30 or 40 is the typical rule of thumb for large $n$. [VI.A.5, VI.C.2]

86. a; From the information provided,

$$\bar{c} = 5.68, n = 32, m = 28.$$

$$\text{UCL} = \bar{c} + 3\sqrt{\bar{c}} = 5.68 + 3\sqrt{5.68} = 12.83.$$

[VI.F.5]

87. a; Note that ranking RPNs works effectively to prioritize corrective action when there is "comfortable" separation between the RPN values. When these values are clustered, the recommended strategy is to eliminate the occurrence to reorder the RPNs, then reduce the severity, reduce the occurrence, and improve detection. [III.E.4]

88. a; A granite surface plate provides better hardness compared to iron surface plates. In addition, granite surface plates are more resistant to corrosion and are less responsive to changes in temperature than iron surface plates. [IV.D.1]

89. c; There are situations where inspection may be considered non-value-added and other situations where it is considered value-added. Inspection of low-cost items, for example, tends to be considered a non-value-added activity. However, inspection of a higher-risk product, or one that is required to be tested by law, could be considered value-added. [V.D]

90. a; The policy statement is the first layer in the manual because it not only provides information about the company's commitment, but policy statements are often provided for each of the applicable standards. [II.B.1]

91. b;

$$\bar{x} = \frac{\Sigma_{i=1}^{n} x_i}{n} = \frac{9.66 + 8.25 + 12.46 + 12.35 + 11.52 + 8.92 + 11.00 + 11.12 + 11.13}{9}$$

$$= 10.712 \text{ V}$$

$$s^2 = \frac{\Sigma_{i=1}^{n}(x_i - \bar{x})^2}{n-1} = \frac{(9.66 - 10.712)^2 + \ldots + (11.13 - 10.712)^2}{9-1} = \frac{4.687}{8} = 2.149 \text{ V}^2$$

The $100(1 - \alpha)\%$ two-sided confidence interval on the population standard deviation $\sigma$ is given by

$$\sqrt{\frac{(n-1)s^2}{\chi^2_{\alpha/2,k}}} < \sigma < \sqrt{\frac{(n-1)s^2}{\chi^2_{1-\alpha/2,k}}}$$

$n = 9$, $s^2 = 2.149$, $\alpha = 0.01$, $k = n-1 = 8$, $\chi^2_{0.005,8} = 21.955$, $\chi^2_{0.995,8} = 1.344$

$$\sqrt{\frac{(9-1)2.149}{21.955}} < \sigma < \sqrt{\frac{(9-1)2.149}{1.344}}$$

$$0.885 < \sigma < 3.577.$$

We are 99% confident that the true population standard deviation of the voltage of the power supply lies between 0.885 V and 3.577 V. [VI.D.1]

92. a; There are nine points in a row above the centerline beginning with the fourth data point. One of the sensitizing rules to detect out-of-control behavior is nine points in a row on the same side of the centerline. Note that a control chart does not provide information on whether the process is operating within the specification limits. A process could be out of statistical control, but still operating within the specification limits. Similarly, a process could be in control, but not be within the specification limits. [VI.F.6]

93. d; The intercept is the value of $y$ when $x = 0$. Therefore, the intercept is –19. [VI.E.1]

94. a; Because the surface of the part is made of aluminum (a nonmagnetic material), liquid penetration testing is most appropriate to detect surface defects. Note that magnetic particle testing can not be used because aluminum is a nonmagnetic material. [IV.D.2]

95. c; The sparsity-of-effects principle is an assumption that is often made that higher-order interactions (orders higher than two-factor interactions) do not have a large effect on the response. This principle is useful when full-factorial designs are conducted with only one replicate. [VI.H.5]

96. a; Since A and B are mutually exclusive, events A and B can not occur simultaneously. Therefore, $P(A \cap B) = 0$. Then $P(A \cup B) = P(A) + P(B) = 0.40 + 0.13 = 0.53$. Note also that probabilities only take on values between 0 and 1. [VI.B.3]

97. b; Power $= 1 - P(\text{Type II error}) = 1 - \beta = 1 - 0.15 = 0.85$, or 85%. Note that the significance level is $\alpha = P(\text{Type I error}) = 0.05$. [VI.D.2]

98. a; The scatter plot shows that as $x$ increases, $y$ tends to decrease, indicating a negative correlation. The points are not closely clustered together, indicating a weak negative correlation. Therefore, –0.39 is the appropriate answer. [VI.E.2]

99. b; Errors in measurement are classified as *random* errors (accidental fluctuations that can not be predicted) or *systematic* errors (for example, operator error, calibration error). Faulty calibration is classified as systematic error. [IV.E]

100. a; This is a unilateral tolerance with variation in only one direction. [III.C]

101. c; The mode is the observation that occurs most often in the sample. In the sample data, a five-minute wait time occurs more than any other observation. [VI.A.5]

102. d; The reliability function is defined as the fraction of all components that have survived for a time greater than $t$. Therefore, the probability that a randomly selected lawnmower will survive longer than $t$ is 4890/5000. Note that the cdf of the failure time $[F(t) = 1 - R(t)]$ can be interpreted as the probability that

a randomly selected unit fails by time *t* or is the fraction of all units in the population that fail by time *t*. [III.E.1]

103. d; The actual capability is the capability measure $C_{pk}$.

$$C_{pk} = \min\left\{\frac{USL-\mu}{3\sigma}, \frac{\mu-LSL}{3\sigma}\right\} = \min\left\{\frac{13.3-10.45}{3(1.05)}, \frac{10.45-8.3}{3(1.05)}\right\}$$

$$= \min\{0.90, 0.68\} = 0.68.$$

Since the capability is less than 1, the process is not considered capable. [VI.G.3]

104. b; Crosby is credited with conformance to specification. Juran is credited with "fitness for use" and Genichi Taguchi is credited with "uniformity around a target value." "Defect-free product" was never a definition of quality. [I.A.1]

105. b; The team would like to test whether the medication errors occur with equal probabilities. Therefore, the null and alternative hypotheses are

$$H_0 : p_1 = p_2 = p_3 = p_4 = 0.25 \text{ versus } H_a : p_i \neq 0.25 \text{ for at least one } i = 1, 2, 3, 4.$$

The significance level is $\alpha = 0.05$. We will reject $H_0$ if

$$\chi_0^2 \geq \chi_{\alpha,k-1}^2 = \chi_{0.05,4-1}^2 = 7.815.$$

The test statistic is

$$\chi_0^2 = \Sigma_{i=1}^k \frac{(O_i - E_i)^2}{E_i}, \text{ where } E_i = (148)(0.25) = 37 \text{ for } i = 1,2,3,4.$$

Therefore,

$$\chi_0^2 = \frac{(22-37)^2}{37} + \frac{(34-37)^2}{37} + \frac{(47-75)^2}{37} + \frac{(45-37)^2}{37} = 10.757.$$

Since 10.575 > 7.815, we reject $H_0$ and conclude that the medication errors do not occur with equal probabilities. [VI.D.4]

106. c; The kilogram, the base unit of mass, is the only base unit defined in terms of a physical artifact, which is made of a platinum-iridium alloy and kept at the International Bureau of Weights and Measures. The definition of the base unit of length (the meter) has changed several times and is currently defined as the distance traveled by light in a vacuum during a time interval of 1/299,792,458 of a second. [IV.E]

107. b; The average run length is the number of cycles, time periods, or samples that elapse before the process signals out-of-control. When the process is out of control, we want the average run length to be small so that changes in the process are detected quickly. If the process is out of control, operators should adjust the process. If an operator does not adjust the process, this underadjustment can introduce additional variation into the process. [VI.F.6]

108. c; A contour plot of the fitted model can help find optimal settings of factors. A contour plot displays the predicted response over the range of the significant factors. Note that main effects plots and interaction plots can also provide useful information in selecting optimal settings of factors. [VI.H.5]

109. a; $\alpha$ is the producer's risk and is defined as the probability that a lot within the quality requirements is rejected. Therefore, the plan has a 1% chance of rejecting a lot that is 2.5% defective. [IV.C.2]

110. d; Since the underlying distribution is normal, the sampling distribution of $\bar{X}$ also follows a normal distribution with mean $\mu_{\bar{x}} = \mu$ and standard deviation

$$\sigma_{\bar{X}} = \sigma / \sqrt{n}.$$

Note that the large sample size requirement is not necessary here since the filling process has a normal distribution. In this population, $\mu = 24$, $\sigma = 0.05$, and $n = 9$. Therefore, $\mu_{\bar{X}} = 24$ and

$$\sigma_{\bar{X}} = \sigma / \sqrt{n} = 0.05 / \sqrt{9} = 0.01667.$$

The probability of interest is

$$P\left(\bar{X} < 23.96\right) = P\left(\frac{\bar{X} - \mu_{\bar{x}}}{\sigma_{\bar{X}}} < \frac{23.96 - 24}{0.05 / \sqrt{9}}\right) = P\left(Z < -2.40\right)$$

$$= 0.0082.$$

[VI.C.2]

111. d; SPC (1) shows when a process is in statistical control (that is, the process variation appears to be random), (2) shows when a process is out of statistical control (that is, the process has nonrandom variability), and (3) can help determine whether or not a process is improving. Control charts indicate that the process is out of control, but they can not identify what caused the out-of-control behavior. It is necessary to identify and correct out-of-control behavior when it is indicated in a control chart. [VI.F.1]

112. b; Consider the bias of the part at each time period. Recall that Bias = Observed average – Reference value.

| Time | Day 1 | 1 month | 2 months |
|---|---|---|---|
| Reference value | 5.00 | 5.00 | 5.00 |
| Observed average | 5.007 | 4.975 | 4.824 |
| Bias | 0.007 | –0.025 | –0.176 |

*Stability* is a measure of how well the measurement system performs over time. In this example, the bias worsens as time elapses, indicating evidence of instability in the measurement system. *Linearity* measures how changes in the size of the part being measured will affect the bias of the measurement system. *Repeatability* is the variability of the test instrument when used to measure the same part. *Reproducibility* is the variability due to different operators or setups of the measurement system measuring the same part. [IV.F]

113. d; The first region of the bathtub curve is known as the "early life" region and is characterized by a decreasing failure rate function. Since the failure rate is time dependent in this region, the Weibull distribution is frequently used to model this region of the bathtub curve. [III.E.3]

114. b; The diagram displays a parallel system with three components. The reliability of a parallel system is

$$R_s(t) = 1 - \left[ F_1(t) \times F_2(t) \times F_3(t) \right] = 1 - \left[ (1 - 0.99) \times (1 - 0.92) \times (1 - 0.95) \right]$$

$$= 1 - \left[ 0.01 \times 0.08 \times 0.05 \right] = 1 - 0.00004 = 0.99996.$$

[III.E.2]

115. a; This is an example of error-proofing, also known as *poka-yoke*. The order will not be processed unless there is complete shipping information and the address has been verified as valid. These extra steps should help reduce errors in shipping. [V.F]

116. b; A *statistic* is a characteristic of a sample and is used to estimate a population parameter. A *critical value* is used in hypothesis testing and is the value to which the value of the test statistic is compared to determine whether the null hypothesis can be rejected. [VI.B.1]

117. d; A fractional factorial experiment uses fewer runs; however, not all interactions of interest may be estimable separately from main effects or other interactions. Some of the effects may be confounded with other effects. This can make it difficult to identify which factor or interaction is actually significant. [VI.H.6]

118. b; If the failure rate is constant (such as when the reliability of the system has an exponential distribution), maintaining the system in an attempt to prevent failures will not affect the probability that the system will fail in the next instant. Therefore, a preventive maintenance policy is not recommended. [III.E.2]

119. a; The *power* of a hypothesis test is defined as the probability of correctly rejecting a false null hypothesis:

$$\text{Power} = 1 - \beta = 1 - P(\text{Type II error}).$$

Type II error is defined as the probability of failing to reject $H_0$ when in fact $H_0$ is false. Type I error is defined as the probability of rejecting $H_0$ when in fact $H_0$ is true. [VI.D.2]

120. c; The scatter plot shows that there is not a linear relationship between the two variables. The correlation coefficient is 0. Note that the correlation coefficient can only have a value between $-1$ and 1. [VI.E.2]

121. a; Given that the lot size is 50,000, the sample size code letter from the ANSI/ASQ Z1.4-2003 sampling tables for normal, level II sampling is N. Using ANSI/ASQ Z1.4-2003 Table II-A, the required sample size is 500. Using the AQL of 1.0%, the acceptance number is 10 and the rejection number is 11. [IV.C.2]

122. d; The necessary conditions for a random variable to follow the binomial distribution are (1) a fixed number of trials, (2) the trials are independent, (3) each trial results in one of two possible outcomes, and (4) the probability of success is constant trial to trial. In this case, we have fixed $n = 50$, the parts are independent, each part can only be classified as defective or non-defective, and the probability of a defective part is assumed to be 0.01. Therefore, the number of defective parts will form a binomial distribution. [VI.C.2]

123. b; Let $X$ represent the diameter of the steel rod. The upper specification limit is 1.58 and the lower specification limit is 1.42. First consider the proportion of steel rods that are within the specification limits, which can be written as $P(1.42 < X < 1.58)$. Since the diameter of the steel rod is normally distributed and the process is stable, we can use the standard normal distribution to determine this fraction. From the control charts, an estimate for $\mu$ is $\hat{\mu} = \bar{\bar{X}} = 1.4983$. The point estimate for the process standard deviation is

$$\hat{\sigma} = \frac{\bar{R}}{d_2} = \frac{0.0906}{2.059} = 0.044.$$

The value for $d_2$ can be found in Appendix C of *The Certified Quality Engineer Handbook*, Third Edition for $n = 4$.

The fraction of steel rods that meet the specification limits is

$$P(1.42 < X < 1.58) = P\left( \frac{1.42 - 1.4983}{0.044} < \frac{X - \bar{\bar{x}}}{\hat{\sigma}} < \frac{1.58 - 1.4983}{0.044} \right) = P(-1.78 < Z < 1.86)$$

$$= P(Z < 1.86) - P(Z < -1.78) = 0.9686 - 0.0375 = 0.9311.$$

Therefore, the fraction of steel rods that are outside the specifications is $1 - 0.9311 = 0.0689$.

Approximately 6.89% of steel rods will fall outside the specification limits. [VI.G.2]

124. d; A tree diagram can take on several shapes. A *fault tree* is used to discover a hierarchical relationship between events that led to a failure in a process. Similarly, an *event tree* defines the relationship between events that lead to a given outcome. A *concept fan* is used during the creative process of finding alternate concepts that achieve the same requirements as a process or product. [V.B]

125. c; When using a double sampling plan, after you take the first sample, you will either accept the lot, reject the lot, or draw another sample. If the number of defective items in the first sample, $d_1$, is less than or equal to the acceptance number, then you accept the lot. If $d_1$ is greater than the rejection number, then you reject the lot. If $d_1$ is more than the acceptance number but less than the rejection number, then you draw another sample. In this case, $d_1 = 6$ and $Ac < d_1 < Re$. Therefore, another sample must be drawn before a decision is made. [IV.C.2]

126. d; Being defensive on a team will quickly defeat the purpose of having a team. It can be overcome with a good facilitator and team leader, as well as a team willing to work together for a higher purpose. [I.F]

127. b; $p$ and $np$ control charts are based on the binomial distribution. [VI.F.5]

128. b; Let $N$ be the event that a nonconforming part is made and let $D$ be the event that a part is made during the day. The given condition is that the part is nonconforming, so we want

$$P(D|N) = \frac{P(D \cap N)}{P(N)} = \frac{5/284}{38/284} = 0.13.$$

[VI.B.3]

129. a;

$$\overline{x} = \frac{\Sum_{i=1}^{n} x_i}{n} = \frac{0.183 + 0.190 + 0.180 + 0.189 + 0.190 + 0.188 + 0.186 + 0.185}{8} = 0.186$$

$$s = \sqrt{\frac{\Sum_{i=1}^{n}(x_i - \overline{x})^2}{n-1}} = \sqrt{\frac{(0.183 - 0.186)^2 + \ldots + (0.185 - 0.186)^2}{8-1}} = \sqrt{\frac{0.000091}{7}} = 0.0036$$

Since the population variance is unknown, and we know that the underlying distribution is normally distributed, we can use a 95% confidence interval with the $t$-distribution. The formula for the $100(1 - \alpha)\%$ confidence interval on the population mean $\mu$ is

$$\overline{x} - t_{\alpha/2,k} \frac{s}{\sqrt{n}} \leq \mu \leq \overline{x} + t_{\alpha/2,k} \frac{s}{\sqrt{n}}$$

$$\overline{x} = 0.186, \quad s = 0.0036, \quad \alpha = 0.05, \quad n = 8, \quad k = n-1 = 7, \quad t_{0.05/2,7} = t_{0.025,7} = 2.365$$

$$0.186 - 2.365\left(\frac{0.0036}{\sqrt{8}}\right) \leq \mu \leq 0.186 + 2.365\left(\frac{0.0036}{\sqrt{8}}\right)$$

$$0.183 \leq \mu \leq 0.189.$$

[VI.D.1]

130. b; An independent contractor not associated with the auditee would be considered an external quality auditor. [II.D.2]

131. a; Histograms are used to understand the shape, spread, and distribution of a set of data. They can, therefore, be useful to compare the data against a target value or specification limits. Scatter diagrams are used to depict the relationship between two continuous variables, Pareto charts are used to identify the most common defects or occurrences in a process, and control charts are used to identify out-of-control behavior in a process. [V.A]

132. d; Let $D_1$ denote the probability that the lot is accepted or rejected on the first sample. Let $d_1$ denote the number of defects found in the first sample. We will accept the lot if there are two or fewer defects noted in the first sample. We will reject the lot if there are five or more defects in the first sample. (Another sample will be drawn if three or four defects are found in the first sample). Therefore, $P(D_1) = P(d_1 \leq 2) + P(d_1 \geq 5)$.

$$P(d_1 \le 2) = \sum_{d_1=0}^{2} \binom{n_1}{d_1} p^{d_1} (1-p)^{n_1-d_1} = \sum_{d_1=0}^{2} \binom{75}{d_1} 0.05^{d_1} (0.95)^{75-d_1} = 0.2697$$

$$P(d_1 \ge 5) = 1 - P(d_1 \le 4) = 1 - \sum_{d_1=0}^{4} \binom{75}{d_1} 0.05^{d_1} (0.095)^{75-d_1} = 1 - 0.6789 = 0.3211$$

Therefore, $P(D_1) = 0.2697 + 0.3211 = 0.5908$. [IV.C.2]

133. d;

$$\text{MTTF} = 115 = \frac{1}{\lambda} = \frac{1}{\text{Failure rate}}.$$

This means that the failure rate,

$$\lambda = \frac{1}{115}.$$

Since the reliability of the dishwasher has an exponential distribution, the probability that a randomly selected dishwasher survives past $t$ months is $R(t) = e^{-\lambda t}$. Therefore, the probability that a randomly selected dishwasher fails by 115 months is

$$F(115) = 1 - R(115) = 1 - e^{-\frac{115}{115}} = 1 - e^{-1} = 1 - 0.3679 = 0.6321$$

[III.E.2]

134. c; The ANOVA table can be used to test for significance of regression. The null and alternative hypotheses are $H_0 : \beta_1 = 0$ versus $H_a : \beta_1 \neq 0$. Note that the ANOVA approach in regression analysis only tests the slope of the regression equation. There are two approaches to test for significance. If the test statistic $F_0 > F_{\alpha,1,n-2} = F_{0.05,1,14} = 4.60$, we would reject $H_0$. Since $F_0 = 52.53 > 4.60$, we reject $H_0$ and conclude that there is a statistically significant linear relationship between the age of the car and its cost. Note also that the $p$-value is 0, which is less than the significance level $\alpha = 0.05$. We again reject the null hypothesis. [VI.E.1]

135. b; From the information provided, $\bar{u} = 0.214$, $n = 28$, $m = 50$.

$$\text{LCL} = \bar{u} - 3\sqrt{\frac{\bar{u}}{n}} = 0.214 - 3\sqrt{\frac{0.214}{28}} = -0.048 \to 0$$

Note that the formula gives a negative value for the lower control limit. By convention, we round the LCL to 0. [VI.F.5]

136. c; The main benefit of an FMEA is that it helps teams to identify and eliminate/ reduce the negative effects of potential failures before they occur. However, FMEA is expensive. Note that FMEA can be used as a stand-alone tool and does not need to be part of a larger quality system such as Six Sigma. [III.E.4]

137. d; *Muda* is another name for waste. *Kaizen* is a performance improvement methodology that emphasizes incremental changes to improve a system. *Kanban* is a visual system that helps to manage the procedure for resupplying tools, components, and so on, in the workplace. *Seiton* is one of the five S's and means proper arrangement. [V.D]

138. c; 100% sampling is appropriate when the fraction of nonconforming products is high. If acceptance sampling were used in this scenario, then most of the lots under acceptance sampling would be rejected, and those lots that are accepted would be accepted because of sampling variability. [IV.C.1]

139. a; The process data in a capability study *must* come from a normal distribution. If the data are not normally distributed, the capability indices are not valid. A histogram and/or normal probability plot can be used to assess whether the process data come from a normal distribution. If the data are nonnormal, a transformation to induce normality may be required. [VI.G.1]

140. b; Selecting the range of factors in an experimental design is extremely important. In this problem, the range of the factor has been decreased. If the range of factors is too narrow, it is possible to miss important effects. [VI.H.2]

141. b; The histogram shows that the data set has a few extremely large values, indicating that the distribution is right-skewed. Left-skewed distributions have unusually small observations. A symmetric, or bell-shaped, distribution has no apparent outliers or unusual observations. A bimodal distribution has two peaks of frequent observations. [VI.A.5]

142. c; As the degrees of freedom approach infinity, the *t*-distribution becomes the standard normal distribution. [VI.C.1]

143. d; Regulatory requirements, customer needs, product or process capability, and product reliability are some of the inputs that will place requirements on the design. [III.B.2]

144. b; The employees have made small, incremental improvements to their processes at the pharmacy. These actions describe *kaizen* activities—incremental changes that lead to small improvements, but improve their process. The changes they have made were simple and did not require expensive technology or equipment, one of the features of kaizen improvement. [V.C]

145. a; Variables sampling plans use the actual measurements of the product of interest. Therefore, these sampling plans determine how close the process is performing relative to specification limits. Attributes sampling plans only tell us whether to accept or reject a lot and do not provide any additional information about the process. [IV.C.2]

146. b; The parameter of interest is the difference in average fill volume, $\mu_1 - \mu_2$. The null and alternative hypotheses are $H_0 : \mu_1 - \mu_2 = 0$ versus $H_a : \mu_1 - \mu_2 \neq 0$. The significance level is $\alpha = 0.10$. This is a two-tailed test, so we will reject the null hypothesis if the test statistic is less than $-z_{\alpha/2}$ or greater than $z_{\alpha/2} = z_{0.05} = 1.645$. The test statistic is

$$z_0 = \frac{(\bar{x}_1 - \bar{x}_2) - \Delta_0}{\sqrt{\dfrac{\sigma_1^2}{n_1} + \dfrac{\sigma_2^2}{n_2}}} = \frac{(15.95 - 16.02) - 0}{\sqrt{\dfrac{0.05^2}{24} + \dfrac{0.04^2}{25}}} = -5.398.$$

Since $-5.398 < -1.645$, we reject the null hypothesis. At the 10% significance level, there is a significant difference in average fill volume between the two methods. [VI.D.2]

147. d; Single minute exchange of die (SMED) is a method for reducing changeover times of machines. It has been attributed to Shigeo Shingo and his Toyota Production System. The goal of implementing SMED is to reduce the time required to switch a machine or assembly to a different product. [V.D]

148. a;

$$\lambda = \text{Failure rate} = \frac{\# \text{ failures}}{\text{Total test time}} = \frac{62}{350 \times 8} = 0.0221.$$

Therefore,

$$\text{MTBF} = \frac{1}{\lambda} = \frac{1}{0.0221} = 45.25.$$

Since the mean time to repair the components is three hours, the steady–state availability of the component is

$$A = \frac{\text{MTBF}}{\text{MTBF} + \text{MTTR}} = \frac{45.25}{45.25 + 3} = 0.9378.$$

[III.E.2]

149. a; Continuous data can take any value over an interval of numbers. Age can be measured on a continuous scale. Gender and hair color are not numeric data. Number of members in the household is discrete data and can only take on certain values. For example, there can not be 2.5 members in a household. [VI.A.1]

150. a; The normality assumption can be assessed from a normal probability plot of the residuals. They should form a straight line in the plot. If the normality assumption is not valid, then a transformation of the response variable may be necessary to perform the analysis. [VI.H.4]

151. d; The second region of the bathtub curve is the constant failure rate region. Since failures occur randomly over time in this region, the failure rate is constant. The exponential distribution is frequently used to model the reliability in this region. [III.E.3]

152. b;

$$E(X) = \mu_X = \Sigma x f(x) = 0(0.86) + 1(0.06) + 2(0.04) + 3(0.03) + 4(0.01) = 0.27$$

$$V(X) = \Sigma(x - \mu)^2 f(x)$$

$$= (0 - 0.27)^2(0.86) + (1 - 0.27)^2(0.06) + (2 - 0.27)^2(0.04) + (3 - 0.27)^2(0.03)$$
$$+ (4 - 0.27)^2(0.01) = 0.5771$$

[VI.C.2]

153. d; Any problem identified must provide an opportunity for improvement. Therefore, to qualify as a performance improvement project, the problem must have variable performance from the established standard, be a deviation from the facts or perception, and its cause must be unknown. If we know what caused the problem, it's not a problem. [V.E]

154. c; Resolution IV designs have main effects confounded with three-factor or higher interactions, and two-factor interactions confounded with two-factor or higher interactions. With a resolution IV design, we do not know for sure that a two-factor interaction is truly significant or whether the two-factor interaction it is aliased with is significant. We may need to add experimental runs to break these aliases. [VI.H.6]

155. d; The population does not have natural groups; therefore, stratified sampling is not necessary for this project. Simple random sampling will allow each customer record to have an equal probability of being selected as part of the sample. Double sampling and sequential sampling are methods used for acceptance sampling and are not appropriate here. [VI.A.4]

156. b; The assumptions for the least squares approach to linear regression are that the errors $e_i$ are independent, normally distributed with mean 0, and have constant variance $\sigma^2$. Note that these assumptions can be verified using residual analysis. [VI.E.1]

157. a; From the information provided, $\mu = 97$, $\sigma^2 = 85$, $n = 24$. The standard error is defined as

$$s.e.(\overline{X}) = \sigma / \sqrt{n} = \sqrt{85} / \sqrt{24} = 1.88.$$

[VI.D.1]

158. a; The floors and room signs match in color to the designated area of the hospital. This is an example of visual control—the added visual cues help patients and employees know where they are in a complicated building like a hospital. [V.D]

159. a; $c$ and $u$ control charts are based on the Poisson distribution. [VI.F.5]

160. d; Let $X$ represent the dimension of the component. The upper specification limit is 13.30 and the lower specification limit is 8.30. We are interested in the fraction within the specification limits. This can be written as P(8.30 < X < 13.30). Since $X$ is normally distributed, we can use the standard normal distribution to determine this fraction.

$$P(LSL < X < USL) = P(8.30 < X < 13.30)$$

$$= P\left(\frac{8.30 - 10.45}{1.05} < \frac{X - \overline{x}}{\hat{\sigma}} < \frac{13.30 - 10.45}{1.05}\right)$$

$$= P(-2.05 < Z < 2.71) = P(Z < 2.71) - P(Z < -2.05)$$

$$= 0.9966 - 0.0202 = 0.9764.$$

[VI.G.2]

Therefore, approximately 97.64% of components will fall within specification for this dimension. [VI.G.3]

161. d; Dodge-Romig sampling tables minimize average total inspection. However, when the process quality worsens, the advantages of these plans are minimized. They also require an accurate estimate of the process average nonconforming in order to select the appropriate sampling plan. Variables sampling plans use actual product measurements to make decisions regarding quality. [IV.C.2]

162. d; Warranty costs would fall under the umbrella of external failure costs. [II.E]

163. c; From the ANOVA table, we can use the *p*-values to determine which factors have a significant effect on the response variable *y*. If the *p*-value < α, then we reject the null hypothesis. If the *p*-value > α, then we do not reject the null hypothesis. From this ANOVA table, the *p*-value for factor A is less than α = 0.05. Therefore, factor A has a significant effect on the response *y*. The *p*-values for factor B and the interaction effect between factors A and B are both greater than α. Therefore, they do not have a significant effect on the response variable *y*. [VI.D.5]

164. a; The takt time for this system is 10 × 60 × 60 ÷ 750 = 48 seconds. The supplier must average one item every 48 seconds. Because the cycle time (40 seconds) is less than the takt time, the supplier is likely to meet the customer demand without changing their current production. [V.D]

165. b; The resolution of a design is equal to the length of the smallest word in the defining relation. Since the smallest word is four characters long in this defining relation, the design is resolution IV. [VI.H.6]

166. b;

| | *x* | *y* | *xy* | *x²* | *y²* |
|---|---|---|---|---|---|
| | 5.2 | 26.7 | 138.84 | 27.04 | 712.89 |
| | 6.1 | 27.5 | 167.75 | 37.21 | 756.25 |
| | 3.2 | 24.9 | 79.68 | 10.24 | 620.01 |
| | 4.6 | 25.5 | 117.3 | 21.16 | 650.25 |
| Σ | 19.1 | 104.60 | 503.57 | 95.65 | 2739.40 |
| Mean | 04.775 | 26.15 | | | |

$$S_{xx} = \sum_{i=1}^{4} x_i^2 - \frac{\left(\sum_{i=1}^{4} x_i\right)^2}{n} = 95.65 - \frac{(19.1)^2}{4} = 4.4475$$

$$S_{xy} = \sum_{i=1}^{4} x_i y_i - \frac{\left(\sum_{i=1}^{4} x_i\right)\left(\sum_{i=1}^{4} y_i\right)}{n} = 503.57 = \frac{(19.1)(104.6)}{4} = 4.105$$

$$S_{yy} = \sum_{i=1}^{4} y_i^2 - \frac{\left(\sum_{i=1}^{4} y_i\right)^2}{n} = 2739.40 - \frac{(26.15)^2}{4} = 4.11$$

$$r = \frac{S_{xy}}{\sqrt{S_{xx}S_{yy}}} = \frac{4.105}{\sqrt{(4.4475)(15.024)}} = 0.96$$

Because *r* = 0.96, there is a strong linear association between the two variables. [VI.E.2]

167. b; In the *forming* phase, an important aspect is developing the mission. [I.D]

168. c; Since MTBF = 8, the failure rate $\lambda = 1/8$. One interpretation of the failure function $F(t)$ is the fraction of all rechargeable batteries that fail by time $t$.

$$F(10) = 1 - R(10) = 1 - e^{-\lambda(10)} = 1 - e^{-\frac{10}{8}} = 1 - 0.2865 = 0.7135.$$

Approximately 71% of all rechargeable batteries will fail by 10 hours. [III.E.2]

169. c; The histogram shows that there are at least two extreme observations in this data set. Therefore, it is most appropriate to use a resistant measure such as the median. The median is not heavily influenced by extreme observations, while the mean is. The standard deviation is a measure of variability/spread, not central tendency. The standard deviation is also not a resistant measure. [VI.A.5]

170. b; Process decision program charts are primarily used to help evaluate a process implementation. They allow a team to assess the implementation plan, identify potential deviations, or develop contingency plans. Activity network diagrams are primarily used to help manage the schedule and timing of a project or set of actions. [V.B]

171. b; Radio frequency identification (RFID) is an effective method for identification and tracking. In healthcare, RFID has been used effectively in patient care by tracking patient movements while they are hospitalized. [IV.B.1]

172. b; Modern training methods were necessary to present new methods to the workforce. [I.A.1]

173. c; Rational subgrouping involves selecting samples such that if there is special cause variation present in the process, there will be a greater probability of variation between samples, while the variation within samples is small. Therefore, the variation within samples is minimized and the variation between samples is maximized. The selection of samples is important when constructing control charts in order to detect out-of-control behavior in the process. [VI.F.4]

174. a; Quality. If we stay with the original perspective experts and customers have when it comes to value (a positive outcome in this case), then quality would be the correct answer. [I.G]

175. d; From the ANOVA table, none of the factors in this experiment have a significant effect on the response. The $p$-values for all main effects and interaction terms are relatively large (> 0.10); therefore, we conclude that none of the factors significantly affects the response. [VI.H.5]

176. a; A one sample $t$-test is appropriate where $H_0 : \mu = 18$ and $H_a : \mu \neq 18$. The degrees of freedom for a one-sample $t$-test are $k = n - 1 = 24 - 1 = 23$. Since $\alpha = 0.05$, we reject $H_0$ if $t_0 < -t_{0.025,23}$ or $t_0 > t_{0.025,23}$. Therefore, the critical values for this hypothesis test (found in a $t$-table) are $\pm 2.069$. Note that the test statistic for this hypothesis test is:

$$t_0 = \frac{\bar{x} - \mu_0}{s / \sqrt{n}} = \frac{17.98 - 18}{0.03 / \sqrt{24}} = -3.266.$$

Since $-3.266 < -2.069$, we reject $H_0$ and conclude that the mean fill volume of soda is not equal to 18 oz. [VI.D.2]

177. a; This is an example of a fail-safe device. Since the components can only be attached to the tool in one way, the tool has been error-proofed from incorrect assembly. [V.F]

178. d; Note that the data are paired since the same component was measured twice, once by each inspector. Therefore, we must use the confidence interval for paired data.

| Component | 1 | 2 | 3 | 4 | 5 |
|---|---|---|---|---|---|
| Inspector A | 10.2 | 9.8 | 10.1 | 10.3 | 10.4 |
| Inspector B | 10.0 | 9.9 | 10.3 | 10.0 | 10.3 |
| $d_i = A_i - B_i$ | 0.2 | −0.1 | −0.2 | 0.3 | 0.1 |

Let $\mu_1$ represent the mean length measured by inspector A and let $\mu_2$ represent the mean length measured by inspector B. Let $\mu_D$ represent the true mean difference between the two populations. $\mu_D = \mu_1 - \mu_2$.

The necessary summary statistics are:

$$\bar{d} = \frac{\Sigma_{i=1}^{n} d_i}{n} = \frac{0.2 + (0.1) + (-0.2) + (0.3) + (0.1)}{5} = 0.06$$

$$s_d = \sqrt{\frac{\Sigma_{i=1}^{n}\left(d_i - \bar{d}\right)^2}{n-1}} = \sqrt{\frac{(0.2 - 0.06)^2 + \ldots + (0.10 - 0.06)^2}{5 - 1}} = 0.2074$$

A 100(1 − α)% two-sided confidence interval on the parameter $\mu_D$ is given by

$$\bar{d} - t_{(\alpha/2,k)}\left(\frac{s_d}{\sqrt{n}}\right) \le \mu_D \le \bar{d} + t_{(\alpha/2,k)}\left(\frac{s_d}{\sqrt{n}}\right)$$

$$\alpha = 0.05, \ n = 5, \ k = n-1 = 4, \ t_{(\alpha/2,k)} = t_{0.025,4} = 2.776$$

$$0.06 - 2.776\left(\frac{0.2074}{\sqrt{5}}\right) \le \mu_D \le 0.06 + 2.776\left(\frac{0.2074}{\sqrt{5}}\right)$$

$$-0.197 \le \mu_D \le 0.317.$$

We are 95% confident that the true mean difference between the length of the components measured by inspectors A and B is between −0.197 and 0.317. Note that 0 is contained in the confidence interval, indicating that we would not reject the null hypothesis ($H_0 : \mu_D = 0$). [VI.D.3]

179. b; Let $T$ represent the time between arrivals at the store. $T$ has an exponential distribution with mean $\mu = 4$ minutes. Since

$$\mu = \frac{1}{\lambda}, \ \lambda - \frac{1}{\mu} = \frac{1}{4} = 0.25.$$

The cumulative density function for an exponentially distributed random variable $T$ is given by

$$F(x) = P(T \le x) = 1 - e^{-\lambda x}.$$

Therefore,

$$P(T > 5) = 1 - F(5) = 1 - P(T \le 5) = 1 - \left(1 - e^{-\lambda \times 5}\right) = e^{-0.25 \times 5} = 0.2865$$

[VI.C.1]

180. b; The number of degrees of freedom associated with the numerator in the $F$-test is equal to $a - 1$, where $a$ is the number of levels of factor A. Therefore, since the degrees of freedom is 5, there are six levels of factor A. Similarly, there are five levels of the blocking factor. [VI.H.4]

181. d; This is an example of waste due to lost creativity. The management at the factory should encourage a quality team to investigate the proposed idea. This could lead to process improvements, and will also increase employee morale as they contribute to performance improvement efforts. [V.D]

182. a; The sample average is

$$\bar{x} = \frac{\Sigma_{i=1}^{n} x_i}{n} = \frac{5.3 + 8.6 + 7.2 + 9.1 + 7.5 + 3.5}{6} = 6.8667.$$

The sample variance is

$$s^2 = \frac{\Sigma_{i=1}^{n}(x_i - \bar{x})^2}{n-1} = \frac{(5.3 - 6.8667)^2 + \dots + (3.5 - 6.8667)^2}{6-1} = \frac{22.2933}{5} = 4.459.$$

[VI.A.5]

183. a; The control limits for the MR control chart are defined as UCL = $D_4\overline{MR}$ and LCL = $D_3\overline{MR}$. The constants $D_3$ and $D_4$ can be found using Appendix C of *The Certified Quality Engineer Handbook*, Third Edition for $n = 2$.

$$UCL = (3.267)(1.75) = 5.72$$

$$LCL = (0)(1.75) = 0$$

Note that the control limits for the individuals chart are:

$$UCL = \bar{x} + 3\frac{\overline{MR}}{d_2} = 17.90 + 3\left(\frac{1.75}{1.128}\right) = 22.55$$

$$LCL = \bar{x} - 3\frac{\overline{MR}}{d_2} = 17.90 - 3\left(\frac{1.75}{1.128}\right) = 13.25$$

[VI.F.5]

184. a; Detecting autocorrelation can be done with many methods, including trend analysis or moving average smoothing. [VI.E.3]

185. c; Dull tools, large changes in raw materials, and a broken machine are all special causes of variation. They are not an inherent part of the process and can be controlled by the operators. Variation in ambient humidity, however, is a natural part of a process, and can not be controlled by the process operators. [VI.F.2]

186. a; The fifth data point is above the upper control limit. One of the rules to detect out-of-control behavior is that one point is more than $3\sigma$ from the centerline on either side. Note that a control chart does not provide information on whether the process is operating within the specification limits. A process could be out of statistical control, but still operating within the specification limits. Similarly, a process could be in control, but not be within the specification limits. [VI.F.6]

187. a; The task of maintaining the risk level below an acceptable level is one purpose of risk control. [VII.C.1]

188. d; The test statistic for a hypothesis test for two population variances is:

$$F_0 = s_1^2 / s_2^2.$$

The test statistic follows an $F$-distribution with degrees of freedom $k_1 = n_1 - 1$ and $k_2 = n_2 - 1$. [VI.D.2]

189. a; The plan–do–check–act (PDCA) cycle, also called the Shewhart or Deming (PDSA) cycle, provides a four-step, iterative procedure for implementing process changes. Total quality management (TQM) is an organization-wide quality program that focuses on customers' involvement in determining quality, employees' obligation to quality, and strong leadership from upper management in quality improvement efforts. Theory of constraints (TOC) is a problem-solving methodology that focuses on the weakest part of a process, and reengineering involves redesigning a process to see large improvements in quality of a product. [V.C]

190. d; From the information provided,

$$USL = 16.75, \ LSL = 14.25, \ \mu = 16.50, \ \sigma = 0.10$$

The process is not centered, so we should use the actual capability metric, $C_{pk}$.

$$C_{pk} = \min\left\{\frac{USL - \mu}{3\sigma}, \frac{\mu - LSL}{3\sigma}\right\} = \min\left\{\frac{16.75 - 16.50}{3(0.10)}, \frac{16.50 - 14.25}{3(0.10)}\right\}$$

$$= \min\{0.83, 7.5\} = 0.83$$

Since the actual capability is less than 1, the process is not considered capable. [VI.G.3]

191. b; Costs associated with spare parts would be under the umbrella of appraisal costs. [II.E]

192. a; The diagram displays a series system with three components. The reliability of a series system is the product of the reliabilities of its components. Therefore, the reliability of the system is

$$R_s(t) = R_1(t) \times R_2(t) \times R_3(t) = 0.99 \times 0.92 \times 0.95 = 0.8653$$

[III.E.2]

193. b; B represents the secondary datum. [III.C]

194. b; While a corrective maintenance policy allows for the maximum run time between repairs, it is not the most efficient or cost-effective. If there is a catastrophic failure, the repair time may be extensive, with high costs. [III.E.2]

195. b; This is an example of waste due to defect correction. The most frequent cause for returns was because the company shipped the wrong item to the customer. The company therefore had to perform rework—process the return, find the correct item, and pay for shipping. [V.D]

196. c; A $k$-out-of-$n$ system design requires that a system made up of $n$ subsystems must have a minimum $k$ subsystems functioning to operate. In this case, since the machine will fail if four of six subsystems fail, the machine has a 3-out-of-6 system design since at most three subsystems can fail before the machine fails. [III.E.2]

197. d; The experiment has $2^{8-2} = 64$ runs. Therefore, this experimental design is a one-fourth fractional factorial design. [VI.H.6]

198. b; *Criticality* is an assessment of the consequences of a failure mode along with how frequently it occurs. [III.E.4]

199. b; *Internal activities* are defined as activities performed while the machine is down. *External activities* are defined as actions done in preparation for a machine changeover. Shingo recommended moving as many internal activities to external activities as possible. [V.D]

200. d; The mean and variance for a random variable that follows a Poisson distribution with rate $\lambda$ are $\mu = \sigma^2 = \lambda$. Given that the standard deviation, $\sigma = 3.04$, $\sigma^2 = \mu = 3.04^2 = 9.24$. [VI.C.2]

201. b; International standards are necessary because they provide a consistent way for interpreting terms, vocabulary, and requirements regardless of language or location of the reader (different languages interpreting information differently was a key problem with standards from different countries and in different languages). [II.C]

202. a; The emphasis is on results; the award is not given for specific products or services, but to reward achievements in quality and performance excellence. [II.C]

203. b; Design review and field trials would fall under prevention costs. [II.E]

204. c; The FTA only uses binary data. This is often considered a limitation of the technique, although the method is very effective for failure analysis. [VII.B]

205. c; The risk priority number is a numerical result from the FMEA. The RPN is the result of multiplying three values: severity of failure, failure occurrence likelihood, and the likelihood of detecting the failure. [VII.B]

# The Knowledge Center
# www.asq.org/knowledge-center

## Learn about quality. Apply it. Share it.

## ASQ's online Knowledge Center is the place to:

- Stay on top of the latest in quality with Editor's Picks and Hot Topics.

- Search ASQ's collection of articles, books, tools, training, and more.

- Connect with ASQ staff for personalized help hunting down the knowledge you need,
  the networking opportunities that will keep your career and organization moving forward,
  and the publishing opportunities that are the best fit for you.

Use the Knowledge Center Search to quickly sort through hundreds of books, articles, and
other software-related publications.

**www.asq.org/knowledge-center**

TRAINING      CERTIFICATION      CONFERENCES      MEMBERSHIP      **PUBLICATIONS**

# Ask a Librarian

## Did you know?

- The ASQ Quality Information Center contains a wealth of knowledge and information available to ASQ members and non-members

- A librarian is available to answer research requests using ASQ's ever-expanding library of relevant, credible quality resources, including journals, conference proceedings, case studies and Quality Press publications

- ASQ members receive free internal information searches and reduced rates for article purchases

- You can also contact the Quality Information Center to request permission to reuse or reprint ASQ copyrighted material, including journal articles and book excerpts

- For more information or to submit a question, visit **http://asq.org/knowledge-center/ask-a-librarian-index**

**Visit www.asq.org/qic for more information.**

# Belong to the Quality Community!

Established in 1946, ASQ is a global community of quality experts in all fields and industries. ASQ is dedicated to the promotion and advancement of quality tools, principles, and practices in the workplace and in the community.

The Society also serves as an advocate for quality. Its members have informed and advised the U.S. Congress, government agencies, state legislatures, and other groups and individuals worldwide on quality-related topics.

## Vision

By making quality a global priority, an organizational imperative, and a personal ethic, ASQ becomes the community of choice for everyone who seeks quality technology, concepts, or tools to improve themselves and their world.

## ASQ is...

- More than 90,000 individuals and 700 companies in more than 100 countries

- The world's largest organization dedicated to promoting quality

- A community of professionals striving to bring quality to their work and their lives

- The administrator of the Malcolm Baldrige National Quality Award

- A supporter of quality in all sectors including manufacturing, service, healthcare, government, and education

- YOU

**Visit www.asq.org for more information.**

TRAINING    CERTIFICATION    CONFERENCES    MEMBERSHIP    **PUBLICATIONS**

ASQ
The Global Voice of Quality®

# ASQ Membership

Research shows that people who join associations experience increased job satisfaction, earn more, and are generally happier*. ASQ membership can help you achieve this while providing the tools you need to be successful in your industry and to distinguish yourself from your competition. So why wouldn't you want to be a part of ASQ?

## Networking

Have the opportunity to meet, communicate, and collaborate with your peers within the quality community through conferences and local ASQ section meetings, ASQ forums or divisions, ASQ Communities of Quality discussion boards, and more.

## Professional Development

Access a wide variety of professional development tools such as books, training, and certifications at a discounted price. Also, ASQ certifications and the ASQ Career Center help enhance your quality knowledge and take your career to the next level.

## Solutions

Find answers to all your quality problems, big and small, with ASQ's Knowledge Center, mentoring program, various e-newsletters, *Quality Progress* magazine, and industry-specific products.

## Access to Information

Learn classic and current quality principles and theories in ASQ's Quality Information Center (QIC), *ASQ Weekly* e-newsletter, and product offerings.

## Advocacy Programs

ASQ helps create a better community, government, and world through initiatives that include social responsibility, Washington advocacy, and Community Good Works.

**Visit www.asq.org/membership for more information on ASQ membership.**

*2008, The William E. Smith Institute for Association Research

TRAINING    CERTIFICATION    CONFERENCES    **MEMBERSHIP**    PUBLICATIONS

ASQ
The Global Voice of Quality